HomesPun Humor:

Original puns, word plays & quips:
A compendium of guffaws, giggles, & mirth

HomesPun Humor

Original puns, word plays & quips:
A compendium of guffaws, giggles, & mirth

David R. Yale

The Pundit of Double Entendres

Author of *Pun Enchanted Evenings,*

Winner of the

2011 Global eBook Award for Comedy & Humor

A Healthy Relationship Press, LLC

New York

Copyright © 2013 by A Healthy Relationship Press LLC New York

ISBN 978-0-9791766-7-8
Library of Congress Control Number: 2013912116

BISAC Codes: HUM004000 HUMOR / Jokes & Riddles
                  LAN000000 LANGUAGE ARTS & DISCIPLINES / General

UK BIC Categories: CB Language, General WH Humor

For additional copies of *HomesPun Humor*, or your favorite Yale puns on T-shirts and coffee mugs, go to www.bestpuns.com/buy1. You'll also find links to buy the eBook version there, as well as Yale's award-winning *Pun Enchanted Evenings: 746 Original Word Plays*.

For information on other pun resources, including books, websites, and Twitter feeds, go to http://www.bestpuns.com/puninfo.html

Follow Yale on Twitter @BestPuns

Interior design by Imago Press, ljoiner@dakotacom.net

PG: Best for Adults Over 18

For Jim Kousoulas

CONTENTS

Introduction
Further Proof That Punsters Are Mentally Superior

This is a book for people who love puns! You may have always suspected that punsters like you are just plain smarter than those sad people who take everything literally and can't understand how a word or phrase can mean two or even three things at once.

My research shows it's true: Punsters are mentally superior!

In my first pun book, *Pun Enchanted Evenings: 746 Original Word Plays*, I cited pioneering studies by Professor Al Gerian in the *Journal of Sighcology* and Professor Sue Crohse in the *Journal of Ego and Id-eology* that showed the personality and career success differences between punsters and people who look down on the art of the double entendre. The findings in a nutshell: Punsters are more flexible thinkers and more successful.

As a result, *Pun Enchanted Evenings* has become recognized as a leading authority by Google Scholar, with the top ranking when you search for *Mental Superiority of Punsters* and *Verbal Dismissal of Puns*.

Google Scholar would have ranked my earlier book as the number one authority on *The Punning Personality*, as well, but it chose to list five treatises on punishment first. Punishment before puns -- what did Google have in mind?

In the three years since I wrote my earlier book, the research on the power of positive punning has exploded.

Professor Sue Crohse of Prince Stun University, in another path-breaking study, has shown that punsters and non-punsters actually respond differently to puns on a physiological basis. Her study appeared in the April 2013 *Anals of Sighcology*.

Looking at the secretion of dopamine, the neurotransmitter that responds to rewarding experiences like food, sex, and rock 'n roll, Professor Crohse found astounding differences between punsters and non-punsters.

When pun-haters heard a pun, their dopamine levels actually plunged, making them feel miserable. "This would suggest an evolutionary maladaption on the genetic level," Dr. Crohse observes.

In pun neutral people, there was no impact on dopamine levels. But in pun lovers, hearing a pun released 1500% to 2500% more dopamine than normal, and making a pun caused dopamine to skyrocket to between 4800% and 7700% above normal.

Or as popular Internet wisdom puts it, "A good pun is its own re-word!"

Looking further into the neurological basis of punning, Dr. Thomas M. Parren MD studied the neurological differences between punning and ordinary speech.

Writing about his work using electronic brain probes in *Advances in Brayin' Studies*, October 2012, Dr. Parren explains that ordinary speech activates between one and two neurological circuits. Hearing a pun, on the other hand, energizes between three and four brain circuits.

But making a pun gets far more of the brain engaged, with six to ten neuron complexes firing away. Unfortunately, this pioneering research has gotten only passing mention in other scholarly journals because they think it's just a Parren thesis! But clearly, it's a lot more than that.

According to a leaked top-secret document from Murky Pharmaceutical Corporation, their scientific team was quick to pick up on Professor Crohse and Dr. Parren's research -- and take it further.

Murky scientists found that Punsters are up to 89% less likely to get Alzheimer's disease. The preventive value varies with the number of puns heard or made per week.

Murky has set up a weekly magazine, *The Punday Clarion-Call*, ostensibly to publish puns, but once Murky buys the copyrights, the puns will become exclusive Murky property, and no actual issues of the magazine will, in fact, be published.

Murky has already paid the FDA commissions that will make it feesible for the puns to be reclassified as a drug, and estimates it can charge $75 per two-pun dose.

Furthermore, the corporation is in the process of hiring 475 litigators to enforce its intellectual property rights. Murky will be the first corporation to license the National Security Agency's database to track down violators of its pun copyrights. "This extensive database will allow us to catch online and telephone violators of our copyrights," said Murky CEO Ima Druggem, MD, in a confidential email to her Board of Directors.

In a sharp break with traditional big pharma practices, Murky plans to recruit doctors into a multi-level marketing organization aimed at selling as many word-play prescriptions as possible.

I dunno, but it sounds like a punzi scheme to me!

But Murky's schemes aside, there is a very real and down-to-earth pun revival sweeping the English-speaking world.

It started with the granddaddy pioneer of them all, back in 1978, the O. Henry Annual Pun-Off, in Austin Texas, which has grown over the years, and now attracts so many participants, entries have to be limited. In 2013, entries reached the limit in a single day!

Of course there have always been books of puns and treatises about punning published. But public get-togethers of punsters have been rare. O. Henry was, for many years, the one, big, well-publicized exception.

But then, starting in 2011, things started to change rapidly. A father-daughter team, she an aspiring comedienne, he a Rodney Dangerfield impersonator, founded Punderdome® 3000 in Brooklyn New York. It wasn't long before they were playing to standing room only crowds, and they found, that with puns, they could get a lot of respect -- and a lot of love, too. Audiences for Punderdome® are so big, they've had to open a satellite show in, gasp! Manhattan!

Around the time Punderdome® was founded, John Pollack came out with his influential book, *The Pun Also Rises,* which draws on history, linguistics, and psychology to explain "How the humble pun revolutionized language, changed history, and made word play more than some antics."

For the first time, pun lovers had hard-and-fast proof that they were, indeed, entitled to respect, based on the myriad of facts Pollack cites.

Soon after this, Angel Leon, a talented bi-lingual punster, founded an online game called Punsr, which has drawn almost 10,000 players from all over the English-speaking globe, including England, Ireland, Wales, Scotland, Canada, India, Australia, South Africa, and the USA. Aside from the sheer fun of it, every pun entered in Punsr becomes part of their online dictionary of wordplays -- probably the largest in the world.

In 2012, London comedienne Bec Hill and friends founded PunRun, which stages pun shows and contests emphasizing humor. It wasn't long before they had to go monthly, because their shows were consistently selling out. And the same thing happened in Minneapolis, Minnesota, where Pundamonium started as a bi-monthly pun slam, but quickly moved to monthly shows because of overwhelming response.

I am pleased to include showcases of the best work of many of these pioneers, right here in *HomesPun Humor.*

If you've been to one or more of these shows, you may wonder why you've never seen me compete. Well, it's true I have written two books of puns. But I just can't think on my feat!

My puns almost never come on command. They just pop up, often at rather inconvenient times. I write them down, and then promptly forget most of them, unless I go back to my pun database and surprise myself all over again when I see them.

But I can promise this: I always strive to follow Rule 9 in Sheridan & Swift's 1719 manual, *The Art of Punning*: " A man must be the first that laughs at his own pun." I do, and I hope you will, too, since I emphasize humor above all else. Because I know that an onslaught of puns that aren't funny can be mirthyless!

I guess it's just the way I'm wired, which has caused me to ask myself many questions over the years:

> I've been wrestling with my problem and its terrible enormity
> And I've finally figured out it's all caused by a deformity
> But I'll put it in plain English so you'll quickly get the gist
> Others were born with a funny bone, but I have a humor wrist!

By the way, names used in these puns are purely fictional. Any resemblance to actual people, other than celebrities and politicians, is purely coincidental.

This book is rated PG, best for over 18. Some of these puns are off-color, which I think makes them even funnier. I know some teenagers I wouldn't hesitate to give this book to. But if you're thinking of giving it to someone under 18, please read it yourself before you give it!

Finally, with the exception of the Showcases, all 823 puns in this book are Yale originals. Or at least I think they are! Great minds think alike, and especially in these days of the great punning revival, it's possible someone else has come up with a few of these wordplays, too.

In any case, I hope you enjoy *HomesPun Humor*!

David R. Yale
New York City, USA, July 2013

1. Cats, Dogs, Birds & Beasts

Daffynitions

Carny-vore: Animal that eats circuses, tents and all!

Piethon: Long, fat snake that loves pastries!

Jeer-raffe: Animal that shouts at and taunts you!

Hypnopotamus: Large African animal that can put you in a trance!

Vege-stable: Where you keep a broccoli horse!

Hiss-tory: A snake's account of his past, spoken in his own words!

Newtrons: Atomic particles unique to salamanders!

Eunoch-horn: What you would call a mythical animal that's sterile!

Rackcoon: Wild animal known to ride on the top of a car with the luggage. Sometimes confused with Mitt's dog!

Duck cling: Why baby web-footed swimming birds hold on to their mothers so tightly!

Skitten: Very young cat who performs short spoofs and monologues!

Opera about the sound of smiling cows: Low-and-grin!

Why are fish so persuasive? Because they take de bait!

What would you call a female deer with no head? I doen't know!

You can't you soothe an agitated flying mammal. Because if you succeed, it'll do calmbat with you!

Fish annihilated by oars in the boating pond are rowed kill!

If you had a prize female pig, and she came down with a serious illness, how would you medicate her? Give her curaçao liqueur!

Why is a particular kind of fish poop unmentionable? Because it's bass turd!

Africa's second largest mammals remember even better than elephants, because in college, they went straight to the hippocampus!

A small fish with a caustic sense of humor is sardinic!

Why do all hogs have eye infections? Every pig has a sty!

What sea animals come looking for you when you jump into the ocean's waves? Seek-you-cumbers!

When told that even small dolphins are highly intelligent, one cynical student said, "I don't know -- it's body seems to defeet the porpoise!"

Where can motherless kittens learn how to become adults? In the Cat-skills Mountains!

Why did the shark talk compulsively after attacking the whale? Because he was a blubber mouth!

What did the injured rabbit say to his wife? Don't worry, I'll recover, hop fully!

Sea lions don't eat sandwiches at their coffee klatsch. They're afraid they have sealy-yak disease!

A parenting error by a devoted mother robin is an on nest mistake!

How does a smart parrot respond to a dumb woman who keeps asking if he wants a biscuit? "Polly wanna crack *her!*"

How can alcoholic birds pry open your windows? They go to the crow bar!

Tika loved her pit bull right to the bit her end!

Pousser cat: French feline that opens doors!

How does a bull know a cow won't have sex with him, just because she's quiet? Because she's not in the moo'ed!

Mama, papa, and baby wolf moved into a brand new 7-room den, with a view of the valley and an attached garage. At first they were very happy, but soon they began to miss the relatives who used to live next door. Mama wolf said, "I sure do miss the old den days!

Merrill the Peril: "I'm gonna bite Bambi!" Mother: "Don't chew deer!"

What would you call a laughing seabird? A giggull!

Why is a brazen kitten's biting toy like a prairie province in Canada? Because it's a sass cat's chew on!

Why is a dog that bites only in the sixth month of the year like an evergreen tree with dark blue berries? Because it's a June nipper!

Did you hear about the 19th century impressionist painter who specialized in strange, monochromatic, cynical portraits of birds? His name was Wrennoir!

A tabby cat mixes her souffle with her whisk-ers!

Why would a livestock scale correctly weigh horses and pigs, but be wildly off for cattle? It needs to be properly cowlibrated!

What would you call a dog with a tiny body and long, long legs? Dispropawtionate!

When dajminish birds fly, they must keep their mouths open to get the extra oxygen they need to move their wings fast enough. So what did the mother bird say to her fledgling before his first attempt at flight? "Beak airful!"

Hogs eat too much out of pignorance!

Chimpanzees always make the high school honor roll because they have an ape plus average!

What would you call a very funny version of a popular song made up by your pet bird? A parroty!

What would you call a cat that insists that its sounds must be flawless? A purrfectionist!

What city and famous song are named for an inflamed bird's foot? Sore wren toe!

What sound does a frightened cat make? A meee-yowl!

Cows low at night when there's mooin' light!

IN THE SHRILL OF THE NIGHT

A very old donkey started hee-hawing one afternoon, and he kept it up without a stop, through the night. That jackass was loud, and the farmer's family couldn't get any sleep.

The next day, the farmer called the vet, who gave the donkey tranquilizers. But the animal just kept on whinnying, just as loud as before. The farmer rubbed him down, but the donkey still bellowed. Even apples and carrots, the jackass' favorite foods, didn't calm him down; he hee-hawed while he chomped on them.

After a week, the farmer couldn't stand it anymore. That donkey was too old to work, so he got his shotgun and aimed it at the beast's head. The donkey took one look, and still bellowing, took off at a gallop, jumped over the barnyard fence, and headed for the woods. Once again, it hee-hawed all night, and nobody got any sleep.

The next day, the jackass was back in the barnyard, still whinnying. The farmer took his high-powered rifle, leaned out the farmhouse window, and shot the critter dead.

The donkey fell to the ground, but a week later, it was still hee-hawing away. The poor animal was brayin' dead!

MOOED MUSIC

There was a man who had an ox who sang wordless songs so beautiful, they brought tears to his eyes. Every day at noon, the ox stood under his favorite tree, and sang until the sun went down.

The man told his neighbors, and they came to hear the ox, but the critter wouldn't sing unless they gave the man money. When they did, the ox serenaded them for the whole afternoon and evening.

People came from far and wide to hear the ox, and pretty soon the man was rich. He loved his singing animal, and wanted to house it properly, so he spent $500,000 building a special house for it. But even with all that money spent, the bovine's house looked, well, quite ordinary. It was, after all, a hum bull home!

He's No Poodull

Some people make their dogs pay for food. I don't believe dogs are personally responsible. If you charge a dog an arm and a leg for a 2 bowls of food, it'll be a paw per! Before my puppy Rex eats dinner, I always tell him, "Bone appetit!"

I have a hard time getting Rex to wear his choker, so I feed him collared greens! It's the leashed difficult solution!

Rex loves fruit, especially pup-paya! And he loves an after-dinner puppermint! Sometimes I give him special foods to motivate him. I taught him to perch on a chair and balance a ball on his nose by feeding him sit trick acid!

When Rex had fleas, I picked them off by hand --not an easy task. You know fleas are fur-tive! Sometimes I feel like his pawsonal assistant! I even have to remind him to keep cool in the summer by wearing his shorts. Otherwise he's always in pants!

Rex is close friends with a young dog next door. Every day, they both do their business, and then spend many happy minutes smelling each other's urine. It's real pup pee love!

The amazing thing is that Rex talks -- but he tells lies. What do you expect -- he's a bull dog! But he loves Microsoft Word files, so he acts like a docs hund!

Rex is a deep thinker. He told me that the opera Madama Butterfly was really composed by a dog named Giacomo Poochini!

When I took him on a cruise, his favorite part was em-bark-ation! There was a big dog with a cask on board. "That guy's master must be an arsonist," Rex said. "That's a St. Burnhard dog!"

But he also has his fears. When we watched a 50s TV show starring a dog, I said she must be very old now. "Don't let that happen to me," Rex said. "Don't let Lassietude set in!"

Even though he can talk, Rex isn't very good at math. One day, I asked, "Rex, how many legs do you have?" "Four paws," he said. "Just forepaws?" I asked. "But what about the back ones?"

2. Health & Fitness

Daffynitions

Voyage ear: Uncomfortable feeling you get in your head when a plane is taking off and landing!

Pebbills: Problems caused by kidney stones!

Henema: Medication for use on a constipated female chicken!

Nigh a sin: Vitamin leads you into ethical transgressions!

Conkussion: Injury you get when a mugger hits you over the head!

Sighatica: Back pain that makes people moan the most!

Hoarsepower: Ability to yell even when you have laryngitis!

Fizzician: Person who heals you with carbonated beverages!

Cope payments: The amount your insurance company makes you pay for psychotherapy!

Backteria: Germs that grow only between your shoulder blades!

The Plenumb: Legislative assembly of the American Board of Anesthesiologists!

Exer-sighs: Sounds people make when they're pushing themselves to work out, but they're really fed up with it!

Soy lesserthin: Food additive to use if you want to gain lots of weight!

Scientists have developed an artificial stomach implant, but it's still intestine stage!

The process of removing all the nutrients from white flour so the bread can look pretty is loafsome!

If you swallow a writing instrument you have to get a pendectomy!

The doctor sent his stomach pain patients to the toy store to buy a colitis-cope!

What's the danger of being overweight and ignoring proper nutrition? You haven't managed to die yet!

When Michael Overby complained of frequent viruses, the doctor told him, "Study French. You'll soon become flu went!"

Many doctors can't diagnose multiple diseases properly. They have trouble with plur-ills!

A woman called 911 for an ambulance and said, "Come quickly! I'm about to give birth." But the child came before the ambulance. It was a case of dial late!

Why did the doctor call in a lawyer to help remove a growth from the patient's face? To make sure he got the de-cyst motion right!

To what does Calvin attribute his amazingly keen eyesight? His Cal-see-um supplement!

What should you take if you're too tense to poop? A relaxitive!

If you eat too many soft, squishy white confections, you'll get a marsh-malowdy!

If St. John's Cathedral had laryngitis, the doctor would tell it to gargoyle with salt water!

Results of a yoyo diet: what you see on your scale fluctuweights!

When someone is tired of being overweight, they have fat-igue!

They police arrested a doctor for insulting hospital attendants. He was charged with diss-orderly conduct!

A man whose arms suddenly fell off and were replaced with ballpoint pens has an overactive limb-bic system!

Did you hear about the two rheumatologists who set up a new practice in town? It's a joint venture!

Awful food for lunch will keep you alert all afternoon because it's un-nap-petizing!

The doctor tried an injection to save the man's life but it was in vein!

Don't let the doctor tap your stomach with his little rubber hammer. You'll have a reflux!

Why do I pee all the time? With age comes whizzdom!

Don't let an 8-year-old run a marathon. Her kid knees might fail!

When you ask a chiropractor when the pain will go away, she says, "Necks tweak!"

Anand Patel thought he was in great shape, so he ran for 5 miles and swam 50 laps. The next day he had a big sore prize!

What would you call a very thin, clumsy guy who just can't put on weight? Ungainly!

How could you tell the doctor specialized in treating senior citizens? She had a medic air about her!

A man lost two-thirds of his rear end in a horrific car accident. Why did he study debate while he was in the hospital? So he could be sure of his rebuttal!

Why don't they play music when they're doing leg joint operations? They're afraid they'll harm a knee!

THE STRANGE MISTER RHEE

When Chester Rhee awoke on his 25th birthday, he had no idea who he was. Total amnesia had wiped out his identity.

His father tried repeating Chester's name over and over, but Chester kept on answering, "That's not me! I have no name."

The only thing he remembered was how to play his violin, so he practiced every day from early morning to late at night, and became a virtuoso.

People loved to hear the nameless violinist, so he traveled far and wide, giving stunning concerts and getting thunderous applause.

After ten years, his manager decided it was time to bring Chester back home for a visit. His friends and family eagerly gathered around. His father asked, "Have you figured out who you are after all this time?" And Chester answered, "Not Chet!"

A GAS TRICK CURE

Mrs. Anderson was troubled with terrible gas, which she couldn't pass. Day after day, she walked around feeling like a balloon. She tried walking, running, and yoga, but the gas got worse. Her doctor sent her to a specialist, who gave her $952.75 worth of pills. None of them helped.

Another specialist insisted surgery would solve her problem. But a month after she went under the knife, the bloating was back.

Desperate now, Mrs. Anderson found a doctor who would take a completely different approach. She was encouraged by his office, which looked more like a café than a doctor's examining room. The doctor, wearing a chef's hat, presented her with a platter of beautifully arranged food that looked like an impressionist painting.

"What's that for?" Mrs. Anderson asked.

"It's a diagnostic test," the doctor replied, "a fine cheese called 'can m'am burp, or do we need a work of fart!'"

3. Family, Kids, Sex, & Relationships

Daffynitions

Base bawl: When a T-Ball player breaks down after he is tagged out at first!

Shower stall: When your 8-year-old son procrastinates about a hygiene task!

Auto-mated: Your spouse was chosen for you by a computer!

Copulate: Fatherhood at age 51!

No-mads: Calmest people in Northern Africa!

Podia tryst: When two feet have an illicit affair!

Ore-gasm: What you get when you make love in an iron mine!

Hollerday: Vacation for people who love to yell and scream!

Fick-illness: What you get from capricious and unstable lovers!

Phallusy: Myth that a large penis makes a better lover

Tepidation: Pervasive fear that someone else showered first, and now the water is only lukewarm!

Belly butt on: Your 3-year-old sitting on your abdomen!

The real reason octuplets are so uncommon is they're 8 typical!

Lucy and Jake had a girl named Mollie, followed by 6 boys. Mollie begged and pleaded for a female sibling, making Lucy and Jake feel terrible. But no matter how hard they'd tried, they couldn't a-sister!

Ella's overbearing mother is happiest when she's explaining what her daughter just said. That lady is in her Ella meant!

Sybil Narishkeit was the apple of her father's eye, his favorite kid who got everything she wanted. When her brother Basil asked for a new car, just like the one his sister had, Pops Narishkeit said no. Basil flew into a rage: "That's not fair! I don't get anything, but everything's Pa's Sybil with her!"

"Why should I respect you?" the teenager yelled at his alcoholic dad. "You're a real faux pa!"

What did the father say when his son asked why the sky is blue? "I have no whydea!"

Why do female praying mantids eat the male after they have sex? To consume-mate their marriage!

Really smart guys ask continual questions to be why's men!

Someone who has perfected the art of nastiness means well!

The tech guy for a singles website is the dater manager!

Young poets go to Love Verse Lane!

A French woman who loses her true love is Je t'aimeless!

The first time two lovers see each other naked, it adds a nude dimension to the relationship!

How can you be sure a new lover will really show up for a hot romantic rendezvous? Make sure he's trystworthy!

If you caution a teenager too much, she becomes warn out!

Back in the 1920s, when it was impossible to get fresh produce in the dead of winter up in Bangor, a pregnant woman craved a salad. "How am I supposed to get that?" her husband asked. His wife answered: "Just roam Maine!"

Why do men think they'll find bliss by viewing porn videos? Because they think it's xxx to see!

Why *should* I stop complaining?" asked the pouting teenager. Her dad said, "Whine not!"

What kind of word game do 3-year-olds play with crayons? Scribble-Scrabble!

For years, the daughter criticized gifts her father gave her, but apologized later. When he gave her an elegant set of gold-plated cutlery on her wedding day, she was annoyed it wasn't solid. Dad finally had enough, and said: "I'll never fork give you again!"

Annabelle and Thomas' baby looks like both of them in every Anna Tom-ical feature!

When the moron got arrested on his honeymoon trip to the capitol of Italy, for shooting water guns at the police, his bride was upset. He shrugged it off: "But honey, I thought it would be so Rome antic!"

Why did the vocalist climb on top of the wedding pastry? He wanted to be the I sing on the cake!

Steve Yakubovich had seven sons. But he wanted a daughter. So when his wife became pregnant again, he prayed to God for a little girl. But when the time came for the blessed event, his wife delivered twin boys. Steve, in a fury, shook his fist at the sky and berated God for not granting his wish. The ceiling of the room suddenly split open, the skies parted, and God, looking down on Steve, thundered: "It is men to be!"

What's the result when a child is able to come between a mother and father? Pair rent!

How can a guy turn a golddigger into a good wife? Give her an anti-"His?? Ta! Mine now!" pill.

Herbie Kaye divorced his wife Louise, who took it hard. She went to the town judge and demanded a decision that she could continue to see all of Herb's relatives. The judge issued a ruling, but it was struck down on Herb's appeal to a county judge. So she went to a state judge who issued a second ruling. Herb appealed to the state supreme court, which told Louise, "You can't have your Kaye kin edict two."

Knot So Fast!

When 6-year-old Bogdan learned to lace up his shoes all by himself, he started to play tricks on his father. He'd sneak up while his father dozed on the couch, and tie his shoes together.

His father, thinking that one of the older kids was pranking him, never confronted Bogdan. But one day, as Bogdan ran off, he tripped on the cat and landed with a thud. His father woke up and roared, "Bogdan! Now I know who's been doing this. No dessert tonight!"

"But Bashta," Bogdan said calmly. "I did knot!"

She Had a Pre-Manition This Would Happen!

Ella Martinez was madly in love with her boyfriend Edward Etienne. She had pictures of him in her silver locket, on the cover of her notebook, on her desk, and on her dresser.

When they weren't together, she wrote poetry about him, and baked him cupcakes. She just knew she'd die if they ever broke up. So she always made sure to tell him, "Eddie, I can't live without you!" Eddie would just smile and not say a word.

But then one day her history teacher asked her to run an errand for him during third period. Ella walked through the hallway and down the stairs, and there, on the landing, was her Eddie, kissing Amanda Auerbach. Ella was right about what would happen. On the spot, she dropped Ed!

SINS EARLY YOURS

Eight-year-old Benjamin Barnstormer was one tough kid, and his family made it worse. His parents actually welcomed his temper tantrums because they had many Benny fits!

He used to terrorize the girls with the dried worms and spiders he kept as creepsakes! And he never admitted doing anything wrong. When his father asked him, "Just <u>why</u> did you break that window, Benny?" he retorted: "No why. Didn't!"

One day he came home with red welts all over his arms and face. "Why did this happen?" his mother asked. He answered, "Bee cause. I threw a rock at the hive!"

By the time he got to high school, he had a very short at-teen-tion span and was very absence-minded! He hung out with a gang that chose its members by their deem meaner!

Even though his parents knew he was a juvenile delinquent, they didn't encourage him to do better. They were afraid he'd become a heartened criminal!

DON'T OVER-ESTEEMATE THEIR HAPPINESS

Low self-esteem problems are part of our genetic heritage, ever since a self-hating primordial protozoan said, "Ah-me, bah!"

People who suffer from self-contempt often admire someone too much and end up feeling awe-ful! Women with low self-esteem get into bad relationships because they have no himpulse control!

Lack of self-assurance is a problem for men, too. A woman can't tell him about all her innermost feelings on their first time out together because she'll intimate date him! And he may demand that she always agrees with him, which makes her bite her tongue and get concur sores!

Repressing emotions is common with low self-esteem people, but it causes major sigh defects! Some couples spend all their time dancing to pulsing, loud music because they're really disco-nnected!

You can't always tell when someone who lacks self-assurance is really unhappy. Many people keep smiles on their faces with a different in tearier!

4. DRINKS & VICTUALS

DAFFYNITIONS

Cruisecous: Middle Eastern dish served on a pleasure ship!

Potpourri: Little pointed spot on pan rim used to transfer liquid!

Potpourri: The person on whom the pan's contents are poured!

Purse-simmon: Fruit that travels well in a handbag!

Awebergine: A 353 lb. British eggplant!

Herbibore: Vegetarian who rambles on about not eating meat!

Cramberry sauce: What students should eat before finals!

Bowlivia: Country where they frown on using dishes at dinner!

Candleoupe: Fruit that gives off light!

Pearsian: Flavor of jam favored in Iran!

Parsnips: Tool for cutting root vegetables!

Pesto sauce: Eight-year-old Merrill the Peril's favorite food!

Buttwiser: Brand of beer smart asses drink!

Penalteas: Types of drinks served to prisoners!

Water crass: Eating this green vegetable causes people to make gross and stupid remarks!

Esca-roll: Baked good made from green leafy vegetable flour!

Apple saws: Sayings about forbidden fruit!

Phyllosophy: The metaphysics of Greek pastry dough!

Pound cake: Pastry made with a big hammer!

Where do you take a sick sandwich? To the mayo clinic!

To avoid broken branches, a plum tree overburdened with fruit sorely needs a good pruneing!

When a tart maker named Francine wins the lottery, it's out of the pieing Fran, into retire!

Street vendors price their food a la cart!

How do people who serve roadkill call their families to eat? "Dinner is swerved!"

What kind of lunch will help inventory takers in a department store quickly count the merchandise? Eye tallyin' food!

What spice is a powerful laxative? Must turd!

If you leave a pot of alphabet soup on your kitchen counter for 4 days, you get a vowel odor!

Why do they drink so much coffee in a Caribbean nation? Because they hate tea!

Adolescents love burgers a lot because they're full of pro-teen!

Chicken farmers track their profits with Microsoft® Egg-sell!

A combination of beer and whiskey makes you feel like playing a kids' game because it's hops-scotch!

Bartenders who pour small drinks with a flourish are dram-atic!

A lack of cravings actually produce an intense yearning for a particular pungent food because it's an un-yen!

What would you call a very noisy evening meal? Din-ner!

A magician who uses a vapor to turn grey apples bright red gives them gas trick a peel!

A neighborhood just outside city limits where they drink lots of beer is the subburps!

Someone who dabbles in pickling spices is a dilletante!

What do legume seeds discuss while they're waiting to be planted? Bean'stalk!

The cook at the greasy spoon got people to praise his omelets because they were egg-salted!

Stew with lots of chunks of beef is out of this world. It's meateor!

Before you eat a Happy Meal,® you must have a Happytite!

When you've worked the plowed earth just before Easter, it's a perfect time to plant Lent tills!

It took a long time for people to realize raisins are a great food because when you look at them, you think, "all dried doubt!"

What would you call someone who bakes elegant little cowpies? A bullshit tartist!

When a customer declines almost every kind of condiment, how does a waitress know what he really wants? Well, the man nays!

What would you say about a child who had nothing to eat but ham and bacon? Pork kid!

City in India with the best pastrami sandwiches: New Deli!

How do top chefs fix broken potatoes? They re-pare them!

Metropolitan area where deep-fried food is popular: Obese City!

There were a bunch of after-dinner candies living in a house. One of them cursed all the time, so the others made him live in the cellar because he was the baser mint!

When Clarence Birdseye invented frozen food, everyone was amazed at this un-can-ny idea!

After hunting, butchering and eating nine deer that were all tough and stringy, the next is guaranteed to be tendeer!

The moron brought a cheeseburger to the hunger strike. He thought it was fast food!

THE POET-TASTER

Joe Bernardini wrote very long heroic poems about legendary heroes, one after another, without any breaks for bodily needs. He grew thinner and more haggard-looking day-by-day, and his best friend Sam Jablonowski got really worried about him.

Sam noticed that every poem Joe wrote had a gourmet feast scene. "Maybe I can distract Joe with gourmet food," Sam thought. But nobody in town knew how to cook gourmet food anymore, and the only restaurants within 100 miles were all fast food joints.

So Sam put an ad for a gourmet chef in the Big City newspaper. To his surprise, a graduate of the Big City Culinary School wrote to him and offered to cook a huge gourmet feast, right there in Sam's kitchen.

The chef cooked for three days and three nights, and Sam went over to Joe's house and demanded his friend come eat. After arguing for an hour, Joe put on his coat and went to the feast. He ate and ate, fell in love with the chef, opened a gourmet restaurant with her, and never wrote another heroic poem again.

It was a real epic cure!

BUT HIS METABOLISM GOT FRUCTED UP

Robert Ekemsi couldn't live without sweets. So when he was drafted, it was a real problem. The army wouldn't serve him second helpings of ice cream because that would be re-treating!

So he got himself trained as a cook, and added sugar to recipes with both hands because he was ambi-dextrose! He even made a soup with salamanders and sugar, which he claimed was very newttricious!

"Why do you drink all that soda?" his commanding officer asked him. Robert answered. "Because I want a good fizzique!"

5. THE OLDEN DAYS

DAFFYNITIONS

Arc-eology: The study of ancient Egyptian geometry books!

Manu-well: Old-fashioned water hole where you use a rope and bucket!

Pill grims: Glum and cranky Plymouth colonists!

Coalonial times: The period in American history when oil had not yet been discovered!

Casills: Malady medieval soldiers got from living in cold, damp stone forts!

Dissaspear: Insult someone's lance!

Well-inforumed: A group of learned Roman senators!

Your royal minus: A very negative king with no personality!

What's another name for the French emperor's skeleton? Napoleon's bony part!

What did Lee Harvey Oswald say to the police before he was shot? "Ask me no questions, I'll tell you knoll lies!"

The king of Thebes was forbidden to operate a chariot because Oedipus Wrecks!

The Knights of the Roundtable wasn't democratically run. It was Arthuritarian.

Ancient Greek buildings replaced themselves by Parthenongenesis!

When the Chinese communists were looking for a leader back in the 1920s, they knew they'd succeed some Mao or other!

When cowboys are herding steer into the pen, they sing corral music!

Invading armies destroyed many Greek and Roman vaulted monuments because they were arch-enemies!

What did the British say about American colonists who helped them during the Revolutionary War? Only laud-a-tory remarks!

We know that back pain was prevalent among the guildsmen of Europe's north coast during the 14th century because they formed the Han-sciatic League!

Which French king was imprisoned, but ate his way out of a stone tower? Louis the Fort Teeth!

The Union army didn't kill the Confederate's leading general at Gettysburg because they didn't use dead-Lee force!

The knights of old carefully collected the corrosion from their spearheads, and gave it to the castle chef. It made great pike rust!

In ancient Rome, the Senate banned chimes in churches, and confiscated them all. But the parishioners re-belled.

Is March 15th really a dangerous day? Ides say so!

The King of Hungary kept the royal pigs in the Magyar sty!

Columbus was a seek captain!

Napoleonic wars were really about toilets. Napoleon was a staunch believer in privies, but the Duke of Wellington gave his all for the water loo!

The biggest problem with turf houses built by 19th Century American prairie settlers was they were wet and sod den!

In the Middle Ages, you could tell what lord a serf belonged to by his manor-isms!

Two viscounts were vying for a promotion. One of them was always late. Why wasn't he promoted? The other was Earlier!

Why was Alkibiades, the Greek, thrown out of the Hellenistic Temple when he said he only recognized the gods Aphrodite, Apollo, Ares, Artemis, Athena, Demeter, Dionysus, and Hermes? He was an eight theist!

They Went to Stirrup Some Trouble

Buck Winslow had wanted to hire two more ranch hands for months, but he couldn't find anyone who was qualified. So when two experienced wranglers showed up at his Double B Bar Ranch, looking for work, he hired them immediately.

The new guys did a passable job, but the day after payday, when Buck went out to check on his cattle, the cowboys were nowhere to be found, the water troughs in their section hadn't been refilled, and the feed troughs were empty.

It wasn't until sundown the next day that the new ranch hands showed up. Buck heard they had been strutting around town, drinking and causing a commotion.

Buck told them they were fired, but they retorted, "Cowboys should be seen and not herd!"

Do it if You Want to Keep Your Job

Alberto de Gonzaga, a 16th Century lesser scion of the famous noble Italian family, ran a huge contracting business specializing in castles.

In 1566, when he got a rush order for a new castle in Guastella from Count Cesare I, he built most of the fortress in record time. But he was still behind schedule, and the eight ornate castle keeps weren't even started.

So he offered four times the normal wages to 10,000 more stonemasons, and told them everything had to be built by sunset the next day.

The leader of the stonemason's guild was aghast. "That's almost impossible," he grumbled.

"Find a way!" de Gonzaga said. "I'm paying a lot of extra money for an eight tower day!"

The Czech is in the Mail

When King Arthur needed to raise more money for the operations of the Round Table, he decided to sell off a plot of land he owned on the town's High Street. But times were tough, and the King couldn't find any buyers. He tried hiring a real estate agent, but that didn't work.

The King grew more desperate, so he delegated the matter to his most trusted knight, Sir Václav Lants, a brave man of few words, who hailed from Prague. Then, the King waited. And waited. For seven long days.

On the eighth day, the King's most trusted knight strode into the throne room, with a new, bright red feather in his helmet and a full suit of armor on.

"Have you achieved your mission?" the King demanded.

"No problem," said the knight. "Sir Lants sell lot!"

Attacked by Knight

Bořivoj I, Duke of Bavaria back in 865, knew that the length of his rule would be determined by the reign god! Nonetheless, he left nothing to chance, and his advanced defense system let him review his huge castle's defenses in just 10 minutes with his moater boat!

Duke Bořivoj always made sure new applicants to his army were not imposters by demanding their sirtificates! Then he gave them a practical test.

That's how he found out one knight couldn't get himself up on his horse with all that armor weighing him down, and just couldn't sir-mount the problem! He also found out this knight lost a battle when his weapon broke -- and he couldn't buy a new one since he had no spear change!

But the Duke was done in by a pre-dawn sneak attack. His enemy camped in the woods and his sentries couldn't see the foe rest for the trees!

6. Communication, Language & Literature

Daffynitions

Infinityve: Verbal tense indicating action that goes on forever!

Ink-comprehensible: Book that can only be understood if written with a ballpoint pen, but never a pencil!

Minglish: Language Americans speak at cocktail parties!

Texastentialism: The official philosophy of the Lone Star State!

Hackademy: Where pulp fiction writers learn their craft!

Inkcouragement: What a timid writer needs!

Addict-ionary: Book of words about drug dependence!

Virgilantes: People who steal copies of *The Aeneid* from libraries and burn them because they think it's obscene!

Legalese: What your knees speak to their lawyer!

Cross sweared puzzle: Word game using only angry curses!

Ode-ious: Very bad lyric poetry!

Semi-coma: Half-conscious effort at punctuation!

Dictatorial monarchs fear the press. They're terrified of break king news!

In what Manhattan neighborhood will you be surrounded very proper English? Grammar Sea Park!

Dr. Jekyll didn't ever drink water. He wanted to become de-Hyde-rated!

Why did they fire the proofreader? They found out she had type-O blood!

Writers of maxims seem to favor one part of speech because they're pro-verbs!

Why did the old time markets use newspaper to package fish? Their customers paid wrapped attention to the news!

Americans understand exactly what the cries of sea birds mean. After all, the birds speak in-gullish!

Which nationality is really into word plays? The Japunese!

Scientists have found that little black insects that meander far from their colonies in search of food actually have a well-developed dialect, linguistically related to Latin. It's definitely a roam ants language!

When the dictator declared words couldn't have connotations anymore, it was de-meaning!

Line Shakespeare would have written about red blood cells reflecting on what they owed their existence to: "To marrow and to marrow and to marrow!"

Truth is that the young hero of a Mark Twain novel was really a peeping Tom. He got his name when someone caught him in the act and yelled, "Saw yer!"

Which philosopher never went barefoot? Sockrates!

The book editor got in trouble when she made un-author-eyes-ed changes!

Richard, the politician, bathed in carmine dye so he would excel at redder Rick!

What would you call malicious lies in a regular feature in the newspaper? Columny!

There's a species of crawling parasites that lives solely on the blood of professors who study language structure. They're called linguist ticks!

Lexicon with no advice about how to actually use the words: Diction nary!

Why did the moron hand in his writing assignments after the deadlines? He thought that would make him article-late!

The Professor Knew His Linguistricks

The City of Mantz was plagued with gangs. Bands of tough guys rambled all over town, spoke their own patois and terrorized tourists.

When one of the packs hijacked a tourist bus and robbed all 77 people on board at gunpoint, it made the international news. After that, tourists stopped coming to see the stunning cathedrals and amazing monuments.

But Professor Ambroos Vermeulen, a language historian from Ghent University, was determined to finish his research at the Mantz Cathedral archives.

Night after night, Professor Vermeulen listened to radio and television interviews with the Mantz gangs, gradually figuring out their unique vocabulary.

When he arrived in Mantz, he was dressed like a gang member. But ten tough guys confronted him at the railroad station, demanding to know who he was.

He answered them in their own lingo, and they were so impressed, they befriended him. One of them worked at the Cathedral, and he gave Professor Vermeulen access to a top-secret archive and told him about arcane historic sites throughout the city.

Professor Vermeulen was free to wander wherever he wanted to, all because he had learned the roam Mantz language!

Rye Bald Cats

Way up in the mountains, there were rare wild cats with beautiful hair which could be made into a stunning yarn -- if you could catch them. For years, nobody could.

But then the villagers realized the cats were visiting their grain fields, and dozing off into deep sleep. So they sneaked up on the cats, and clipped their hair. It was a cat shear in the rye!

THE POET WAS NOT A-MUSED

Darya Kozakova was a frustrated poet who was trying to write fiction. She had completed her first book, *Ocean Storms*, but couldn't get started on the next novel, *Sea Quell!*

"But you're a beginning versifier," her friend Elizabieta told her. "Amateur poets can't write fiction because then they'd be prose! Besides, your first novel is a dead giveaway that you're a poet."

"And why is that?" Darya demanded.

"It's full of very long run-on sentences. They make readers commatose! Stick with your poems. I like your word plays in iambic puntameter!"

"But Elizabieta. Why can't I get going on my second novel?"

"Darya, that's because you live in a one-story house!"

So Darya went back to writing poetry. But she was having trouble paying the bills, especially when the poetry journals came up with a scheme for paying poets by the couplet, which was especially per verse!

She knew that poets will rule all the galaxies someday, because they're masters of the you know verse!

But meanwhile, her poverty was making her very angry, so she took a job as a dominatrix and made a big name for herself.

Her specialty was speaking in verse while cracking her whip. Clients came from far and wide to experience her whacks poetic!

7. Psychology & Success

Daffynitions

Pre vent: How you can avoid a temper tantrum when you begin to feel anger building!

Self phone: For getting in touch with your id without going through psychoanlaysis!

Diss-connected: Clinical term for a couple who do nothing but hurl insults at each other?

Ass-ass-innate: Person who's inherently doubly asinine!

Cup ills counseling: Where two married mugs go when their marriage problems are making them sick!

Toe-bias: What you should never call your child if you don't want him to become a foot fetishist!

Correspondance: When two lovers write long letters, but can't get to the point of true commitment!

Skitsophrenia: One actor with 2 roles in funny theatrical sketch!

Happen stance: Yoga pose that reorganizes your energy so you can get things done!

Grin-ade: Explosive smile!

Awethentic: Genuine astonishment!

Did you hear about the woman who always made socially inappropriate remarks? Her psychiatrist finally concluded her sense of propriety was not in tact!

Symptoms when something is bothering you subconsciously: You get idtchy!

Why are people in dysfunctional families so attached to each other? Because of their guilt-edged bonds!

When a person doesn't believe they really exist that's an nillness!

Irish song about cheering up a depressed person: When Irish sighs are smiling!

The most important factor in a proper greeting: good hellocution!

When teaching writing to agitated people, psychologists advise you instruct them to use lots of punctuation because it's supposed to make them comma!

Schizophrenics are great billing clerks with all their in voices!

What would you call a psychiatrist's examination of an uptight person who gives way too much attention to detail? Anal-ysis!

If your sister's daughter is bashful, what should you serve her? Oh, maybe egg rolls and wonton soup, you know, shy niece food!

A depressed person who permits himself no joys in life and spends his time in a dark room has turned off de-light!

What happens to type A people when you take away their organizational tools? They become listless!

Stanley Kapliades was a high achiever, a millionaire by the age of 25. A reporter asked him how he managed to do that. "I have very high Stan dids," he answered!

A carpenter in an anger management class wouldn't remove the insect from one of his tools. He didn't wanta fly off the handle!

If you grew up on a mountain top you may be unable to think in a flexible manner because you have a ridge id!

Why would an overcoming fear audio CD never succeed? Because people using it would be disk couraged!

He Really Needed a Self Phone

Kenneth Aagard and Emma Hjelle were high school sweethearts, and now that Ken had gone away to college while Emma stayed behind to work at her dad's grocery store in New Ulm, he was having a hard time.

When he couldn't decide whether to take French or German, he called Emma. Should he buy a grey or black winter coat? Another phone call. Had he really studied hard enough for his biology midterm? He was on the phone again.

Even after he got his first phone bill for $285.20, he couldn't stop calling her. By the end of the semester, he couldn't make any decisions, no matter how small, without consulting Emma.

"Should I have roast beef or chicken for dinner? Should I pay for my dry cleaning with exact change or break a twenty? Should I walk behind the student center or along the quad to go to my dorm?"

He hated his indecisiveness, but he couldn't stop calling. It was all a real dial Emma for him!

He's Just an Ill Lucian

Six-foot-tall Lucian Harding was a dashing young feller, clean-cut, with black hair and a model's good looks. He got lots of first dates with gorgeous women, but it never went further.

"At first they seem to swoon over me," Lucian told his shrink. But by the end of the evening, they're reading every text they get and going to the ladies room a lot."

"Hmm. Very interesting," said his shrink, fingering his goatee. "What do you talk about?"

"Well I love talking about my matchbook collection. That and antique beer cans are my favorite topics."

"Ah," said his shrink. "I know what the problem is. You have a dis-awed her!"

DISS SATISFACTION

Fifteen-year-old Frankie the Mouth broke into a bookstore to steal an oak bookshelf, but it fell and pinned him to the wall. The cop who arrested him said, "Looks like there's quite a case against you!"

The judge sentenced him to probation and sessions with a social worker who tried to find out why gang members like Frankie can't stop their provocative expressions of disrespect.

"Duh! Because when we stop, we diss-continue!" Frankie said. "We have to insult each other. You may think we're terse and clipped, but we're really being curteous!"

"But you're all diss connected. Keep it up, and you'll be diss abled, Frankie!"

"We ain't any different than them talk shows where the hosts ignore facts and make personal attacks on anyone who disagrees with them. They don't have any response-civility either!"

"Frankie, this is like a contagious diss ease! But there is a better way. I want you to attend some for-ums -- You know, the opposite of against 'ems! If you're negative all the time, you'll get nope place in this world!"

So Frankie went to the for-ums, and his probation officer got him an apprenticeship with the electricians' union. He became less cynical and had a great awe-titude!

One day, the social worker's uncle came to visit him, but he got lost, so he stopped and asked a man working at the top of a lamp post for directions. "Yes sir, I'll come right down and help you out," the man said. "My name is Frankie."

He drew a map for the visitor, and even thanked him for coming to the city. Later, his Uncle told the social worker how impressed he was.

"Of course," said the social worker. "That's my friend, Frankie. He's on the pole light crew!"

8. Business, Banks, Corporations & Finance

Daffynitions

Sumday Best: What inventory takers wear for an extra day of weekend overtime!

Hire-o-glyphics: Coded writing on employment applications, designed to disguise age discrimination!

Flacks seed: Used to grow PR people!

Cog-itate: Think about your place in the corporate machine!

Cog-nizant: Having thought about your place in the corporate machine, you fully understand it!

Reap hay: What you must do if you borrow against your silage crop!

Savery: Thrifty person's favorite spice!

Bearometer: Instrument for measuring negative stock market sentiment!

Penny-ten-tiary: Where would you end up if you stole a dime!

Hocktober: National credit card month!

The most important skill for management success is super vision!

Critical skill for an income tax preparer: Deductive reasoning!

Al Asaro graduated from high school, and started working in the family business. But it wasn't long before he began to criticize the way his mother ran things. So she fired him. The moral of the story is, "Pan a ma, can Al!"

What do retailers hope to do when the recession is over? Some ka-ching up!

Why did Anna McCann's performance figures never quite add up? Because when she interprets them, Annalyze!

Why do the best workers in a printing plant get fired first? They're ink competent!

Estelle Okonkwo had a very soft voice. What did she do to make sure she'd be heard at a critical business meeting? She used Esty Louder cosmetics!

Did you know Charles Darwin wrote a book about the invention of gold coins? Yep, it's called "The Origin of Specie!"

Insect colony with lots of small businesses: Free anterprise!

Jaded bill collector to new apprentice: "Been there, dunned that!"

The PR executive hired the young graduate with no experience because of her hype potential!

The annual inventory at a beer company causes more injuries than any other activity because it's brew tally thorough!

How do we know big corporations despise customer phone calls? They say your call will be answered in the ordure it was received!

Did you hear about the mining company that tried to get stimulus funds to bulldoze a scenic mountaintop and strip the coal underneath? They claimed it was a shove hill ready project!

The new branch manager, sent over by the head office in America, didn't speak German, and was nasty, demanding, and impolite. The German staff got so angry, they took him to court where the judge ruled he had to say "please" in German. It was a bitte pill for him to swallow!

Romney's financial program for America was eco-NO-metrics!

It took years to change British currency to the decimal system, but proponents succeeded because of their ten-acity!

Why did the guy with no hair enjoy it when his boss yelled at him? Because he wanted to get bald out!

Bankers who set up investments bound to fail, so they could bet against them and make billions, should be put in jail with just their shorts!

Which Eastern European monarch invented the most common form of paying bills before online payments came along? King Samo was ahead of everyone else in 623 AD. He had a Czech King account!

Why is systematic cutting of wages and benefits as hard to understand as exotic mathematics? Because it's a buy nary system in a consumer driven economy!

When big shopping centers come to town, ma & pa stores get malled!

Lawyers are like cats. They like to get their clause in everything!

Stupid salespeople selldumb close a deal!

"Now Gina," the manager of the medical office said to the new assistant. "I gave you a hundred urine samples to go to the lab. Did you package them all up and get them all dispatched?" "Yes m'am," Gina answered. "One hundred piss sent!"

What you must never say to a boss who is harassing you: "Will you lay off?"

A bright new coin loses its luster from all the hand dulling!

When she was buying her first house, Melissa Lewin's lawyer warned that the deed went way back to the 1900s and had some weird clauses that are now universally ignored. "Like what?" she asked. "Well it says you may not keep a horseless carriage on your property." "That's really in there?" she asked, incredulous. The lawyer said, "In deed, it's so!"

To quickly find gentrified neighborhoods, Search by latte-tude!

Americans prefer houses with basements. In fact, they're best cellars!

Learn How We Do It Ore Else!

Worthington Jones III, the newly-appointed CEO of Dungus Metals & Minerals Extraction Corporation, wore his usual luxuriously-tailored suit, fitting for a Harvard MBA, to his first meeting of the company's executive team.

They were a scruffy bunch, wearing blue jeans and tee shirts, but he'd have to work with them -- at least for now -- even if they were impossibly old and behind the times. They spent money hand-over-fist, and they paid the workers way too much, but he'd take care of that really fast.

"Johnson, the Engineering Department's safety budget is way too high. I want your written plan to cut it by 25% on Monday," he thundered. Johnson looked amused, but he didn't say anything.

At the Monday meeting, Johnson handed his report to the CEO. It consisted of five pages, all blank.

"Why is there nothing here?" the CEO bellowed.

Johnson answered, "Jones, never you mined!"

De-lighted by Bad News

Anand Chatterjee's whole family knew he couldn't think in daylight. So they always waited until well after sunset to ask him anything. And if it was really important, they chose a cloudy night with no moon.

But one day, right at high noon, the postman delivered a letter notifying Anand that the bank was foreclosing on his house because his last payment was a dollar and twelve cents short.

"What are we ever going to do?" his family wailed.

Anand stood up, walked over to the windows, pulled the heavy wood coverings closed, and drew the shades.

"This is a crisis," he said. "I shutter to think about it."

THE BANKSTERS' PORTFOOLIO

I don't like banksters, but I feel sorry for them. They feel friendless because they always loan sum! They're dejected, desolate, despairing and despondent because they pinch every penny and hoard their money which tends to make them miser-able!

But you can't trust them. When you go for a loan, they encourage you to fill out an app-lie-cation! Then their agent overstates the value of your house because he's an upraiser!

To make a mortgage payment, you have to go to their cash shearer! Even if it's a debt you regret, they have that promise, sorry note!

No wonder those psych loans blew apart the housing market! But the banksters tried to solve the real estate bubble with salt water because they believe in the sale lien solution!

Banksters have lavishly catered private parties where they dream up new ways to grab your money. They call them fee-estas! When you go to a meeting with them, better take a fee-nix bird with you! And if they're trying to sell you toxic sickurities, watch out! They use a special color called chart ruse to present a graph of misleading financial figures!

They think they're masters of the universe, and their credit card bills are like the holy book because they're buy bills! Did you know that banksters have their own god? Back in 2008, banksters came from far and near to worship at the feet of Obadiah Widdity. In fact, they paid millions of dollars to lick Widdity!

But I think they're insects. In fact, if you look at the side of a banskster's head, you'll see a fine ant's ear!

That's why I really got a kick out of the news story about the guy who stole a hundred balloons from a bank, filled them with water, and threw them at the window. He got a bank wet at their expense!

9. SPORTS, LEISURE & RECREATION

DAFFYNITIONS

Brawl game: Sporting match where all the fans start fighting!

Goaled medal: Highest Olympic honor for hockey players!

Stilt on: Type of cheese eight foot tall clowns eat!

Pie a la mowed: You tripped and dropped an ice cream pie on your freshly-cut lawn!

Socke: What Japanese boxers drink!

Iran: Where long distance sprinters retire!

Trivial purse suit: Frivolous legal action alleging a trademarked handbag design was copied.

Par king lot: Golf course designed to make you win!

Entrée form: Paperwork to get your main course recipe into a cooking contest!

Leisure: Certainty the football player will accept the flowered festoon!

Polyeaster: Synthetic material made only for Lenten clothing!

Quizzine: Food served during a game show!

Lawngevity: Health effect of cutting the grass with an un-powered mower!

Why did the moron stay in the dark place beneath the bleachers when the Yankees played? He wanted to under stand the game!

When a football star marries a tennis champ, do they pro create?

A cynic in the well known Florida theme park might be arrested for dis-awe-derly conduct!

People go to Las Vegas to gamble so they can feel bettor than everyone else!

It's hard to focus while running track. Your attention will laps!

Michelle Kwan's desk is in her off ice!

If you caught a fish that swallowed your best lure, would you de-bait it?

Why won't adding equipment help a gardener become more efficient? Because the task just gets lawn gear and lawn gear!

Someone who needs lots of water is like a board game when he tries to hike in the desert, because he'll parch easy!

What kind of soap does Santa use to wash his suit? Yule Tide®!

What did the Yankees coach say to the new player from France? "Europe next!"

Steer don't play baseball because it would be all bull's hit!

How much more food does an NFL Quarterback need than an ordinary guy? Pro-portion-ately more!

The Great Lakes look really similar. Sometimes you can't tell what Lake Huron!

I saw that famous tower in Paris. It was a real eyeful!

I actually saw a woodsman slay a charging grizzly with just a small, shiny piece of glass. It was a mirror kill!

A company that sponsored skipping and dancing contests for children was shut down. The police said it was a gamboling joint!

Make sure you appreciate your lawn work. Live in the mowment!

How can you tell when it's Christmas Eve? Yule know!

Fisherman, after a great catch using artificial bait, thank the lured!

Why can't you predict if Tiger Woods will win his next tournament? Because it's never a certain tee!

What would you say to someone handing you a line about having been a professional football player?
"I've had enough of that pro feign language!"

The judge made Lawrence buy 100 Yankee flags as a penalty for sneaking into the Stadium. He wanted Lawrence to pay pennants!

Why did the mountain guides put down the baggage when they lost their way? They wanted to get a load down on the situation!

What do very picky people say when they refuse to use an uninspiring toilet? Too dull loo!

The Lewis County High School girls' fencing team always won because it had great team spear it!

Did you know they used to play charades at the big estates in the south before the Civil War? They called it plantermime!

How do you know when a gardener is disgusted? She'll throw in the trowel!

Why will your daughter have a lot of holiday spirit if you name her Christina Melissa? She'll be Chris Missy all year 'round!

What nutrient should be served 3 times a day to minor league players? Pro-team!

The Mississippi State crew team has to put up warning signs on the river when they practice because they're doing rowed work!

You can't climb to the top of a volcanic mountain in Hawaii because no matter how much you climb, you never leave Mauna Lower!

And if You're Really Worried, Get an Ex-Tension Cord

Darla and Joe bought a huge, dilapidated Victorian house under a century-old oak tree near downtown. They had big plans to replace the old roof and rattling windows, update the kitchen and bathrooms, sand the floors, and scrape and paint the walls.

The day they took title, they turned on the electricity, and soon an acrid smell filled the air. Darla found three outlets that were hot to the touch, so they called an electrician.

Five hundred dollars later, the electrician pronounced the problem cured. But two days later, the master bedroom and hallway lights started to flicker, and the acrid smell was back.

They brought in a different electrician, who charged them $800, and said everything was all right now.

But a week later, all the lights in the dining and living rooms were out, and changing the fuse didn't help.

A third electrician charged them $1200 to fix that problem. Alas, a few weeks later, there were more hot outlets, flickering lights, and the master bathroom had no power at all.

Still another electrician rewired the problem areas, and billed them for $3000. But a month later, sparks flew and the kitchen lights went out.

Then there were electrical problems in the basement, the guest room, the attic, and on the porch. Thousands of dollars later, the problems kept returning.

"Looks like this is too much for the electricians," said Darla.

"What are we going to do," asked Joe.

Darla thought and thought, and came up with the perfect solution. "Let's hire Derek Jeter. He's the best shorts stop!"

That's Knit a Gift

Every year, Anika Naaktgeboren's mother gave her husband Joris a hand-knit sweater. The old lady sat and knit for hours, making sure each stitch was perfect.

But Joris didn't appreciate the sweaters because they weren't store bought. And in his mind, that meant they weren't really gifts.

Joris would open his mother-in-law's present, look at the intricate patterns knitted into the wool, frown, and say to his wife, "No gift. Just a cardigan!"

10. Getting There –
Planes, Trains, Cars, & Boats

Daffynitions

Rolled Royce: Luxury car upside down in the ditch!

Boatox: What you rub on an old, puckered and crinkled yacht hull to make it look new again!

Cabooze: Moonshine brewed by freight train crews in the olden days while on the job!

Cartunes: Songs sung by an animated mouse's auto!

Junk bonds: Funding needed to buy a very old, exquisite example of a high-sterned Chinese sailing boat!

Ha-choo-choo train: Thomas the Tank Engine® with a cold!

Co-oar-dination: The most important skill for two people rowing a boat together!

Gone-dola: Stolen Venetian boat!

Honky Tonka®: Metal toy truck with a working horn!

How was Captain Sullenberger able to successfully land his disabled aircraft on the Hudson River against all odds? Because of his superior grasp of herodynamics!

When Louisa started getting seasick, her dad told her to look at the place where the sea meets the sky and keep horiz-on it!

Did you hear about the trucker who was fined $15,000.00 for being a single pound over the load limit? He said it was high weigh robbery!

Why can't a brightly-colored taxi transport packages? Because it wouldn't be a dull livery vehicle!

When the railroad conductor checks your ticket, he's looking to see if it's valid dated!

Why were there so many dumb people on the overcrowded bus? At every stop, they tried to get more and moron!

When the city came up with new traffic rules, it was so hard to change driving directions, you had to go from here to u-turnity!

What kind of frost forms on two-wheeled vehicles in winter? Bicicles!

A male passenger on Flight 500 took off his clothes just before the airplane landed. What did they charge him with? In descent exposure!

How did the trucker know there was a problem with his load of live poultry when he entered the Windy City? He heard an illy noise from his chick cargo!

A teenager went up to the car wrecking concession at a London street fair, watched as people paid a quid to hit an old car with a sledge hammer, fished in his pocket and found only 50 pence. "Would you give me a go for this?" he asked, showing his coins. "Sure!" said the concession owner. But you only get half a pound!"

Father to teenage son driving too fast on a slick, wintry road:
"Slow down!"
"Why?"
"Because ice say so!"

The Captain assigned a particularly lazy sailor to clean up the Lido Deck before the passengers boarded. An hour later, when the Captain came by to inspect, the sailor whined, "Ain't it time for a break, Cap'n? I've been here a deck aide!

What's the ideal name for a used vehicle saleswoman? Car-lot-a!

What would you call a bobblehead likeness of a reality TV personality, designed for installation on the flat surface under your rear-view mirror? A Kim Car Dashian!

When the oven on the ship stopped working, and the crew was demanding cooked food, what did the captain do? He hit a rock and stove in the boat!

Why don't bedbugs bite taxi drivers? They taste too livery!

In the old days, who could diagnose a locomotive's mechanical problems just by listening? The engine ear!

What would you call a cruise with a huge amount of gourmet food? A bloat trip!

When a man makes a solo trip across the Atlantic Ocean in an oar-powered boat, what does he get at the end of the journey? A he rows welcome!

Did you hear about the new plug-in car from Japan? It's called the Honda a cord!

Factory owners find large increases in railroad freight rates tarrifying!

SUSPENSE-FUL WAITING

Back in March, 1923, on an unseasonably warm day, a city slicker in an expensive blue suit was driving a Hispano Suiza Cabriolet de Ville along a rutted dirt road through hardscrabble tenant farm country, his silk tie flapping in the breeze.

He drove up a hill, and came to a long flat area, where the road looked pretty decent, so he shifted gears and sped up.

He drove into a wooded area, and before his eyes could adjust to the sudden dimness, he hit a boulder in the road with a loud crack and an awful sounding sprong!

The car stopped in its tracks, and tilted sharply to the right. The city slicker got out, took a look, and even though he was no mechanic, he could see that he had broken his suspension.

After several hours, a farmer came along in a horse-drawn wagon, stopped, looked the situation over, and said, "I'm going to town next week. I'll order a new suspension for you."

"That's a long time to wait," the city slicker said.

The farmer thought a while, and said: "Cheer up. Spring is coming!"

Going Faster Wagon His Tail

When a group of settlers were crossing the Mojave Desert, one of their wagons hit a bad rut, and the whole front end broke.

Everyone was upset except Abner, a talking dog who was really good with his paws. Abner found a few stunted desert trees, cut them down, and replaced the broken parts with better ones. The wagon was much easier to steer when Abner tested it.

All the other grim-faced settlers were perturbed by Abner's joy, and asked him how he could be so happy. He exclaimed, "I just invented rack and piñon steering!"

He Put a Stu Dent in the Car

Seventeen-year-old Stuart Connors was taking his first driving lesson in the snow when the car went into a skid. The instructor grabbed his steering wheel, and tried to pull out of it, but Stuart panicked, turned <u>his</u> wheel the wrong way, and they sideswiped a garbage truck.

When the constable arrived on the scene, he asked Stuart and his instructor what happened. They both talked at once, and it was hard for the constable to figure out what they were saying.

Finally, the Constable said to them: "Let me get this straight. You were *both* driving, co-wrecked?"

AMERICAN DRIVERS ARE NOT WELL-TRAINED

Once upon a time, every American city had trolleys. But the oil, rubber, and automobile corporations hatched a plot to destroy America's streetcar lines, and they got away with it because they covered their tracks! When they burned down the trolley buildings, it polluted the air with a lot of carbarn dioxide!

Now we have buses, which have more accidents from distrackded driving! Don't ride them through the mountains except during rush hour. You don't want an off-peak bus!

People don't like buses, because they're never sure when they might be detoured and where they have to get on. Some of them jump on the roof because they think that's where the bus top is!

Bus drivers are notoriously out of shape. In the old days, trolley car drivers got lots of exercise. They ran track!

Now, Americans are up-to-date, and we take responsibility for our own transportation. We've become a real carnation!

Even I finally bought my own car. On my first road trip, the gas pedal got stuck. I swerved to avoid a beaver, and hit the guardrail, which caused a bad road-dent! I felt the problem was caused by flaw mats, but the car-maker denied it because they didn't understand the relationship between cause and defect!

I took my car to an auto body repairman, who made a lot of caustic jokes because of a more dent sense of humor! Disgusted, I drove to the dent-ist, who went next door to a deli, and bought some slices of car-patch-io to fix the fender!

When I needed new tires, I drove to the service station. A young lady looked over my car. She was shy and retiring! I pointed to my worn treads and asked, "Can you put a new outside on these?" But I got no re-ply!

My car is really smart, with all those computers built in. So it decided to write an auto biography! And it even tells me how to avoid hazardous roads with detailed dire wreck shuns! I like that. I'm less likely to have an accident and an angry faultercation!

11. Art, Design, Music & Magic

Daffynitions

Humonyms: Songs with the same sound but different meanings!

Bela Bar Talk: Hungarian composer who loved to chat in Irish pubs!

Twerpentine: Solvent you get from stunted pine trees!

Assthete: Sculptor who specializes in butts!

Art decko: Mural painted on a ship's floor!

Mediochre: Poorly drawn oil painting with too many yellows!

Slaps tick: Comedy about someone tormented by blood-sucking insects!

Comety: Funny play about an astral body!

Credit card: Comedian who jokes about borrowing money!

Tap dancing: When water waltzes out of the faucet!

Dosi-dosage: Pill for people who can't square dance because they have two left feet!

LiLoGo: Lindsay Lohan's trademark!

Sackbutt: Instrument played before announcement that all knights were being laid off at the end of the crusades!

Brew grass: Music you play while you're fermenting lawn clippings to make hard liquor!

Bandtering: Small talk among brass players!

Cymbal Simon: Game percussionists play!

Sing-a-pore: Where all the people have musical sweat glands!

I-Tunis: Website distributing North African music!

Clap-board: Type of siding performers like on their houses!

What are the best hues to use in the illustrations in a history book? Past tell colors!

The apex of Chinese choral music was the Sung Dynasty!

Designers should use Halvatica type for Turkish candy wrappers!

Why did the magician push down on the end of his assistant's foot just before he pulled a rabbit out of his hat? Because the assistant said, "Press toe!"

Why did the famous composer's daughter go crazy when she got married? She un-Raveled!

What would you call a flat broke person panhandling for carfare to get home? Waiting for go dough!

They keep huge vases with abstract designs on them in the Museum of Mod Urn Art!

Did you hear about the magician who waved his wand and a huge table appeared, loaded with a sumptuous dinner, waved his wand again, and it was gone? He called it his dis-suppering act!

Why did the chorus director feel free to goose the singers? They were singing a canticle!

Upholsterers don't hum about their work. It's too tack sing!

Why did the moron paint the Mona Lisa on the screens on his house? He wanted to have Louvred windows!

Workers always sing about the same thing in the ballpoint factory. They have a pen-chant for it!

They couldn't raise the price on old-time nickelodeons, even when massive inflation hit. They were mechanickel devices!

Librarians like marching bands because they're in formation!

Scientists just found an extremely rare art print form the Stone Age. It's called a paleolithograph!

Where did they used to sing dirty songs in the Catskills? Gross Singers Resort!

The jazz band that tried to save money by eliminating the big stringed instrument found that de-bassed the music!

Nine pins players love Ravel's Bowlero best!

Why did the ancient Greek potters gently slap their huge vases after they put the glaze on? To get pat urns on them!

The Count had sculptures installed in the ditches around his castles back in 1780 to get some original moats art!

Instrument you play barefoot: socks-off-phone!

What did the writer say when asked how the play he was writing would end? "That remains to be scene!"

The Chinese emperor's awkward son burned his dad's antique 15th century carvings so he could be prince char Ming!

Why is Albert Auerbach so mathematical when he dances down the street playing the tuba? Because he has an Al go rhythm!

Some women excel at singing in the shower. They're sopranos!

The art song really flowered under German liedership!

Why is a man with tattoos all over his upper trunk like a piece of furniture? Because he has a chest of draws!

Walls in an old house make music when the paint is pealing!

The orchestra fell on hard times, so the conductor did a public survey to find the cause. "It's the percussion section," he determined. "We have to do something drastic to get us out of the dull drums!"

The Yuletide log sang in harmony because it was chord wood!

All highly gifted macramé artists are poor. They have knots!

A big dot and a little dot are the opposite ends of the specktrum!

An eagle that plays piano with its claws has great talont!

What kind of music do the best baseball hitters listen to? Swing!

Music is truly a global language because it's intonational!

Buck King Up Royally

The king of comedians went to an old-fashioned dude ranch in the Colorado grasslands. On his first morning, he wanted to go riding but there were no horses available right then.

"Whaddya mean?" he said to the wrangler. "Ain't these grey ones here horses?

"No sir, those are jackasses. And they'll make a jackass out of you if you try to ride them. They buck worse than any horse," said the wrangler.

But the comic insisted on riding a jackass, so the wrangler saddled one up and the funny guy mounted.

The royal comic didn't go more than ten feet before he went flying through the air and into the ditch.

The moral is: "A mule and his funny are soon parted!"

No Longer a Step-Brother

Back in the 1950s there were two half-brothers, Joe and Nick, who wrote do-wop music and sang it in the neighborhood streets.

One day Joe came up with a song that he was sure would make the top 10, so he sang it for Nick, who got all excited and started yelling, "You're right! This is gonna be a huge hit, Joey boy!"

But before Joe could sing it in public, Nick gathered a crowd on the front steps of their apartment building, and sang it a capella.

Everyone in the neighborhood loved what they called "Nick's Song," so Nick, emboldened, hired a band and recorded it -- without Joe. Pretty soon it hit number one on the charts.

Nick avoided his family, but Joe finally cornered him and said, "I can't believe you would stoop solo!"

She Was Toast

The director of the Golden Valley Contemporary Music Festival walked into his new assistant's office and glowered.

She was supposed to be working on commissioning a major composer for the featured piece, but there she was drinking champagne. He never would have hired her if he had a choice, but her father was a well-connected big donor, so it was grin and bear it.

"Why aren't you working on getting that commission assigned?" he barked. "You only have a few weeks left."

"Sit down, sit down," she said, handing him a champagne flute and the bottle. "Phillip Glass!"

Next Thing She'll Have Her Own Aukestra

Marianne "Ma" King, the great barrelhouse pianist, played to packed houses in small deep-south clubs. The years passed, and Ma raised six kids, tended the garden and chickens, but always had time to rock the house on Saturday nights.

Everybody said, "Ma, how come you ain't famous yet?" but Ma just loved the music, and didn't think much about getting on the radio and making records.

When she was 68, a man wearing a fancy suit said he could get her a recording contract. But she didn't believe him.

"Yeah, sure," she said. "I'll sign that contract when you name a bird after me, young feller."

To her surprise, the young man said, "Sure thing, Ma'm. I knew what you were gonna say. That bird's already named after you. It can listen to your music, and then repeat every note you play."

"What kind of bird is that?" she asked.

He replied with a grin, "A Ma King Bird!"

AT PARTIES, ALWAYS ON THE PUNCH LINE

Before comedy existed, in the pre-hysteric era, someone had to invent it! One guy rolled his bread into little spheres, and threw them across the room, trying to create rye balled humor! Another aspiring comic use a car wheel for a chair so he could write sat tire!

But Joe King, the first successful comedian in recorded history worked with a demolition crew to learn their secret. Because they always brought down the house!

Once he learned the formula, he taught a college class on bawdy humor. It was a popular coarse offering! Joe was also the first humorist to understand that a corny comic delivers the punch line by ham-mering the point home, and he often used lighted candles in his act, to be wick-edly funny!

But the years were tough on him. Because sad, but true, he found out that experienced humorists aren't as funny as they once were, because now they know laughing matter!

HE NEVER GOT A BOO-QUET!

A devilish young onion worked hard to become a hip-hop musician. People said he was a real rapscallion! But he actually studied all kinds of music.

To get into the best college pop music program he had to fill out a rock enroll form! He listened carefully to the wind in the meadow because it blew grass! And he managed to get ahold of Count Basie's autobiography, even though it was a band book!

True, he did get into a big brawl once, by infuriating a baroque choir who were all experts at Bach sing! And he got arrested for performing a new ditty in public!

But audiences loved him, and he finally got the recognition he deserved when Goldman Sachs invited him to lead a secret, high-level finance sing!

12. Nature, Weather & the Environment

Daffynitions

Scorchair: A blisteringly hot day!

Peakuliar: Strange mountain top, usually after strip-mining!

Forkcaster: Someone who tells the weather with pronged silverware!

Squall talk: Meteorologist chit-chat! If they're throwing challenges at each other, they're full of hot dare!

Minuwet: Dance under a waterfall!

Al Gore rhythm: Mathematical proof for global warming, set to music!

Why did the fields turn bright cobalt colored after the typhoon? Because the wind blue so hard!

In what Middle Eastern country do the rulers hate precipitation? Bah! Rain!

What must you never plant on a green roof? Leeks!

What California city gets the most rain? Torrance!

How many tons of cement in a mile of 4-lane freeway? I dunno. Ask the road weigh!

What would you call a plan to generate electricity from chicken manure? Recapturing henergy!

Why did the moron plan a car trip for the middle of a hurricane? He thought it would be easier to travel during a driving rain!

What would you do if you were caught in the garden by a flash flood, you had a boat, but you didn't know how to use the oars? I'd ask a rows bush!

A strong wind tore all the sharp points off the bushes in the rose garden. It was a thornado!

What medical problems does industrial pollution cause? Chemickills!

Why do people avoid electricians restoring power after storms? Those linemen are re-volting!

A snow man in warm weather is thawmented!

When the hurricane blew the windows off the meteorologists' headquarters, it became a storms enter!

What would you call it when a diver gets goosed by an octopus? A tentickle!

Why did the moron climb the mountain to do his math homework? He thought he'd do better at the summ-it!

What do you get if you cross a reptile with a stinging insect? A bee-lizard!

Why is an earthquake in the city so musical? Because it rocks tar!

Did you know that if you pee in the ocean, you get more sea weeweed!

Did you hear about the train that used waste biomass from a spice factory for fuel? It was always running on thyme!

A polluted reservoir has H_2 woes!

Why is global warming a critical issue? Because rising oceans present a real emergent sea!

UNDEWING OVERDEW PROBLEMS

Two rain gods spent the whole night practicing ballet so they'd have a perfect pas de dew! But then they overslept and mist the train to their appointment. So they dropped little round ice balls on a yellow taxi to hail a cab!

They finally got to their lawyer's office, and asked him to hire a collection agent to handle all the past dew bills! "The Tea Party took over governing the heavens," they told their lawyer. "So we'll also have to hire an econo-mist!"

"Cut back on your expenses," their lawyer told them. "One of your apprentices is a real extreme mist! And that other one who spends hours placing each drop of the morning mist -- tell him not to be such a dew fuss!"

"And make your refreshments with two cups of mist so they serve double dew tea!"

The rain gods replied, "Dewly noted!"

INN SIGNIFICANT FLOOD

I was a little disappointed by the country inn, in a small river town in Western Connecticut. Sure it was quaint, but it also looked old and faded. The roof needed patching, and the siding desperately needed to be scraped, sanded, and re-painted.

But the innkeeper gave me a cordial welcome. My room was clean, comfortable, and well-furnished. I could hear birds chirping in the garden, and breezes rustling the trees.

After a day of hiking the hills surrounding the river, I came back to the inn famished. The innkeeper served me a banquet, with venison, squab, roast chicken, new potatoes green beans from her garden, and my choice of three home-baked pies for dessert.

As I drifted off to sleep that night, I heard distant thunder. But the day's hiking had tired me out. I fell into a deep sleep.

I was awakened by someone shaking me as the first light of a grey dawn crept into the room. Rain came down in solid blocks.

"River's rising. It's gonna flood. Quick! We have to get out!"

The other guests and I followed the innkeeper, up a winding road to a huge house on a bluff hundreds of feet above the river.

"We can stay here until the flood's over," the innkeeper said.

We could hear the angry torrent's roar below us. I watched as it leapt over its banks, and quickly covered the town. Only chimneys and weather vanes were standing above the roiling waters.

By late afternoon, the flood had subsided. We walked to town to see how bad the damage was.

What a surprise! The houses all looked freshly-painted. The clapboard on the inn seemed brand new. And the roof looked like it had just been installed.

"How could this be?" I asked the innkeeper.

"Oh," she said, shrugging her shoulders. "It's just the House-a-tonic River!"

13. Farm, Factory, Crafts & Trades

Daffynitions

Bangle ore: City where they get all the raw material for jewelry made in India!

Lost-and-foundry: Where they recreate missing machine parts!

Cowculus: What dairy farmers use to figure out the quantity of hay needed to feed the herd!

Beet-ills: When a virus-carrying insect nibbles on the red root vegetables!

Cowlamity: What you would call it if a tornado blew the doors off the dairy barn, leveled the fences, and the animals were wandering the woods on the back 40!

Bee-reaved: How the farmer felt when all the honey-making insects in his hives died!

Steeroids: Medication you give a castrated bull with a bad case of inflammation!

Ponderous: Why you can't move the farmer's small lake!

Carpenterr: Correct name for a miscalculation when framing a new house!

Boarding school: Where millwrights learn their trade!

Collarships: How apprentice shirt makers pay for their training!

They are very strict about safety in the factory where huge bolts of white cotton are colored, so nobody is allowed to tell jokes on the job. They don't want anyone to dye laughing!

Things look really glum for farmers with bumper crops of legumes because that makes them has beans!

The moron planted grapes in the wheat field because he was raisin' bread!

Harvesting grain is very boring because it's so reapetitive!

Why wouldn't they let farmers into the game show audience? They're from the hint-erlands!

If a carpenter lost her electric tools and she needed to cut a lot of wood pieces, she'd have to get a hand sore!

How do you weave air mattresses? On a family airloom!

What's the risk when you use fake granite in your kitchen? You'll have a problem with counter fit!

The farmer tried to protect his granary from mice, but it was all for gnawed!

You can't nail into the part of a plank where a branch used to grow. It would split and wood knot work!

What do you say to a swarm of unruly honey-making insects? Beehive yourselves!

The seamstress who couldn't get Superman's costume right after seven tries was not very cape-able!

Why can't Joe King's son ever become a plumber? Because his name is Lee!

How do they say goodbye at a cut-it-yourself Christmas tree farm? Thanks for chopping with us!

What did the farmer sing to his field early in spring? I hadn't anyone till you!

What is the best wood Gepetto could have used to make his puppet? Pin oak, you know!

How would you color leather black with just a gas? Use carbon dye ox hide!

What nickname would you never give to an electrician? Shorty!

The entire warehouse staff of the A&B Cookware Company was hauled off to jail for pan handling!

When the old farmer's equally old mule wouldn't haul the wagon one day, he gave it a dose of may-pull syrup!

How do you harvest winter wheat by hand? With an icesickle!

How come carpenters never carry flashlights, but they can always find things in the dark? They have seek lamps in their tool boxes!

The seamstress promised she'd finish my daughter's prom dress, but when I checked today I saw it was not sew!

What did the plumber say to his apprentice when they were trying to close an ancient valve that looked very fragile? "Be careful! Don't faucet!"

When the formidably expensive cashmere yarn became hopelessly tangled in the knitting machine, none of the factory's workers could untangle it. So they called in an expert, who said, "Knot a problem!"

When the unemployment counselor suggested the jaded ex-farmer should go back to agriculture, he said, "Bean there, done that!"

Why did the farmer call the fertilizer store at midnight?
He wanted to get nightrates!

Potters wear a lot of lipstick and mascara because they're always into make cup!

The pastor of a very ornate church, with 4 towers, asked a contractor to bid on painting the exterior. When the bid came in, it seemed very high, and the priest asked for an explanation. The contractor responded, "It's very hard work, and we charge per spire!"

The secret of efficient hay farming is slow mow shun!

When the farmer saw that all his hives were empty, he didn't bee leave it!

Does it take much time to tailor a dress? It seams sew!

Tailor to apprentice: "I'm afrayed that un-hemmed edge won't last!"

AND YOU SHOULD SEE THEIR CARRION LUGGAGE

A pair of magpies built their nest in a farmer's attic. The farmer didn't know it, but magpies are notorious thieves, and this pair were champion crooks.

At first the farmer didn't mind, but they stole every bright and shiny object they could find and put it in their nest. The farmer began to get annoyed.

One Sunday, the farmer was having a party in the dooryard to celebrate his 25th wedding anniversary. The table was set with the family's best china and silverware. One of the magpies swooped down, grabbed a silver spoon, and flew off with it, leaving the farmer and his family swearing and grumbling.

That night the farmer crawled into the attic to search the magpies' nest for the spoon. The stench from dead mice and birds the magpies had collected for food was overwhelming.

The magpies awoke, screeched, and attacked the farmer with beaks and claws, leaving bleeding cuts and welts all over his arms. That nest had become a huge birdden to him!

A DEADICATED WORKER

Nate Coleman was working on a machine in the foundry when it jammed. The foreman came along, and ordered Nate to push as hard as he could on the feed bar. Nate pushed until his face turned red.

"Don't break the feed bar," the foreman yelled. "Now hurry up and get this machine unstuck. We're losing money every minute."

Nate pushed harder, the veins in his face swelling up and turning blue. Sweat poured down his face, and his arms trembled. The feed bar began to bend.

Suddenly, the feed bar popped free, the machine started running again, and Nate fell down dead.

The foreman shrugged and said, "Better Nate than lever!"

Appealing Sound

When the beloved 12th Century bell in the Mantz City Hall tower cracked, the Mayor sought far and wide for someone who could repair it. All kinds of artisans and craftsmen looked at it and said, "It can't be fixed. Replace it."

But the citizens were adamant. "We want *our* bell, not a replacement," they demanded.

Three years after the bell cracked, an old woman knocked on the Mayor's door.

I hear you need a bell repaired," the woman said. "I'm sure I can repair it. May I see it?"

The woman and the Mayor climbed up the bell tower. She stroked the bell, and tapped it with her knuckles.

"I can fix it, guaranteed. It will cost you 5,000 Euros."

The mayor agreed, and the woman went to work. Twenty days and twenty nights later, the bell was repaired, and its sound rang joyously over the town.

The Mayor handed the woman her check. "How can I thank you?" he asked.

The woman grinned. "Just nominate me for the Know Bell Prize!"

In a Dark Prison Cell, Tom May Never Get Releaf

Tom the Tree didn't like the feeling of heavy fruit on his branches. So before it could fully ripen, he twisted and turned and shook it all off.

The young fruit was furious, and called the Juvenile Protection Unit.

The police came, Tom was arrested, and taken to court. The judge ruled he must be tried by a jury of his pears!

A VERY CAPE-ABLE FOX

Obadiah Jones was a tough old farmer, who had killed many a fox trying to raid the chicken coop. But lately, a particularly sneaky critter had broken into his coop, and made off with three of his best roosters.

The farmer knew that foxes usually struck late at night, after the moon had gone down. So he went to dinner without a worry, and arrived at the chicken coop well before the moon waned.

"I'm gonna blast that varmint clear out of creation, and I'm gonna do it tonight," the old man said to himself.

All was calm as Farmer Jones sat with his 30-30 rifle across his lap. The crickets sang, and gentle summer breezes blew, but there was no sound of a fox to be heard.

But Freddy the Fox was waiting, too. He had snuck into the coop while the farmer had dinner, killed a young rooster, and was waiting until the moon went down to make his getaway.

Half an hour after moonset, Freddy slung the dead rooster around his neck, eased out of the coop, and started running.

Farmer Jones thought he heard something, but he didn't see anything. He jumped up and started firing his rifle.

Freddy doubled his speed, and didn't stop running until he was clear across the barnyard, over the meadow, into the woods and deep inside his den, where his wife and children eagerly waited for their chicken dinner.

The old farmer never even saw Freddy zoom across the barnyard. What was Freddy's survival trick?

He had a black capon!

14. EDUCATION

DAFFYNITIONS

Lessen plan: Guide for teaching school kids how to subtract!

Pettygogy: How to teach insignificant details for standardized tests!

Un-collegist: Doctor academics go to when they want to come down from the ivory tower and get back to reality!

Gabberdeans: Clothes worn by college administrators who love gossip!

Eelective: Advanced fish recipe course at Japanese cooking school!

Kin-degarten: First year of home schooling for triplets!

Water course: College class on the geology of streambeds!

Class sacked: When all the kids in fifth grade pitched in to fill sandbags before the hurricane came!

Why do some French students limp? They go to the Sore Bone!

Why did the high school principal discourage individual tutoring sessions? He felt that it lessons your ability!

People who want to cut back school budgets won't take "know" for an answer!

What did the teacher say when he caught a student cheating, and took away credit for the final exam? "I de-test you!"

Why do students get so upset these days if they get one grade less than an "A"? They don't want to be B-rated!

A college president insisted the pillars in every fence on campus must be enrolled in a post doctoral program!

Standardized testing leaves no time for inspiring wonder. There is now severe awesterity in our nation's classrooms!

What was the most serious college in America, where even laughter was prohibited? Anti-yock in Ohio!

Did you hear about the Irish kid who graduated from Sixth Class in a tiny one-room schoolhouse in the countryside near Derry? That didn't meet government requirements, so he had to get a Second, Derry education!

Time-travelers brought teachers from 1929 to visit a classroom in 2010. They looked at the whiteboard and said, "Re-markable!"

Why did the school principal invent a dance for groups of 10 students and make them practice it endlessly? He wanted a ten dance that was perfect!

What kind of school doesn't penalize you for missing an exam? A cosmetology school has lots of make-up tests!

The strict English teacher forbid the use of contractions in both written and spoken usage. When students violated this hard-and-fast rule, they were charged an apostro-fee!

Someone drew little brown bugs all over my math textbook. They ink roached on my property!

Professors survived the great flood on knowers ark!

Students against the over-use of standardized exams can't express their opinion. Because when they do, they're pro-testing!

She Finally Got the Point!

The kids in 8th grade hated their teacher, Miss Mezquindad, who delighted in making them cry in front of the class.

One Monday she made fun of Sara de Arellano because she didn't like the girl's braids. Sara, mortified, ran sobbing from the classroom. Her boyfriend, Samuél Fuerte, swore he'd get revenge.

Samuél bided his time, waiting for the right moment. On Wednesday, when the teacher left the room, Samuél put a tack on her chair, carefully painted to match the wood, so it was almost invisible.

Miss Mezquindad started toward her chair, and the whole classroom went totally silent. But even though she sat down hard, there was no reaction from the teacher.

Later, when the Miss Mezquindad left the room again, the kids found the tack was squashed flat. Samuél went home that afternoon and prepared a stronger, denser nail.

Again, Samuél waited for the right moment. Finally, late on Friday afternoon, the teacher left the room for a moment, and Samuél carefully placed the new nail on her chair.

Miss Mezquindad soon came back, sat down, screeched — and keeled over, dead.

"Oh my God!" the kids screamed. "Samuélito gave her a harder tack!"

A Very Mr. Rios Set of Circumstances

Harlan Rios was a very popular math teacher at Milton High School. After 43 years, he had a perfect attendance record, a sheaf of awards and commendations, and no complaints in his file.

But one day in May, he vanished into thin air. His briefcase was found in a local orchard, and the farmer heard someone yelling insults at the fruit, but found nobody there. The moral of the story is don't revile a fruit or *you'll* diss a pear!

TRYING TO GET INTO THE HIRE-ARCHY

When my son Joe graduated, we knew his high school digree might not even get him a job shoveling manure! I mean, these days, you even need a mast-ers degree to build sailboats!

So we figured he'd better go on to college so he'll learn more money!

We wanted him to avoid those party schools that emphasize skoalastic achievement! But we also didn't want him to study excessively, and never take a break, because that really gets you fact up! Besides, with his level of test-o-sterone, we knew he'd do OK!

But when we got our first bill from his college, we knew paying it would take plenty of two wishin"!

Finally, the big day came, Joe got his diploma, and looked for a job. He applied for a position as a bankcur filling sacks with money at Goldman! But they said, "Grad you wait!"

He had to stand in line for two weeks, just to get an in turn ship! When Joe asked for his salary, the boss said, "Be pay shan't! Some day, you'll get corpo-rations!"

So Joe got a night job at a laundry. Not much of a challenge, and he was going nuts ironing bored! But at least it paid the rent for his tiny condo-minimum!

He finally got a decent job at a bridge building firm, working for Mr. Brett. It really helped that Joe spoke Span-ish! He learned very quickly that you must use a pencil to draw a level rule. If you use a pen, you get an ink line!

Joe got to be real good at finding mistakes, and could immediately spot a problem with a blooperint!

He thought he was doing really well, but his boss gave him a box of dried grapes when Joe asked for a raisin pay! Of course Joe smiled, but it was really a sha-grin! My son knows what side his Brett is buttered on!

15. Cops & Robbers

Daffynitions

Inntruder: Burglar who specializes in small rural hotels!

Con-cept: Idea that's larcenous at heart!

Lootenant: Army officer who steals money from civilians!

Skulldiggery: When grave robbers dig up human heads to turn into souvenirs!

Thuggestion: Advice from a mobster!

Con-sensus: When 100 crooks agree on the best way to pull off a heist!

Arsonic: Chemical a criminal uses to burn down buildings!

Horse-iffer: Another name for a mounted cop!

Cop pout: When a police officer meets a question with a sullen frown and no answer!

A man stole two headdresses from a market in southern India. He was arrested for dis-turban the peace!

How did you get away from those kidnappers," the police asked the 6-year old. The kid answered, "Ran some!"

Why are parolees forbidden from using two walking sticks, but one is OK? Because they're not supposed to use co-canes!

What color hair does an arsonist have? "Aw, burn!"

What city has the stiffest penalty for peeping toms? Peeks kill New York!

Suggestion on a mob hit list: Highly recommendead!

The millionaire couldn't walk after thieves stole his black fur coat. He was dis-sabled!

If you commit a minor offense in the African city of Port Louis, you get charged with Mauritius mischief!

What did the seasoned mobster say to the novice who was nervous the body they were about to dump in the ocean would be discovered? "Just weight and sea!"

Why are dumb swindlers so prevalent at the beach? Because of all the silly-con dioxide in the sand.

A 7-year old girl was arrested for bringing her popsicle-stick covered crafts project into a bank. They thought it was a stick cup!

When Gabriel Smith was accused of stealing his neighbor's house keys he said, "Finders keypurse!"

The bank robber in a backwater town was told by the judge that the only way to appeal his conviction was to see Justice Vail. But when the robber was taken to see him, he discovered that it was really to Noah Vail.

AP-PEAS THEIR BEEFS

Inmates 32016 and 88575 went to the new warden at Bleak Rock Penitentiary on behalf of the Convict's Association to complain about his severe new austerity measures.

"The new coats aren't heavy enough. And you've turned the heat so low, I'm always cold," said 32016.

"Me, too," said 88575. "I feel like my bones have turned to ice."

"The new small soap bars don't last through the week. I can't get really clean," said 32016

"Me, too," said 88575. "I always feel grimy and gritty."

"I need more than just potatoes to eat. I'm always hungry," said 32016. "Where are the vegetables?"

"Meat, too!" said 88575.

And Then the Nasty Judge
Looked at Him With Penaleyes

Kensington Wentworth was walking down Fifth Avenue, minding his own business when he tripped and landed with a thud. Two cops arrested him because he fell on knee!

They took him to a brand new police station, and he wanted to wash his hands, but he couldn't because it was the pre-sinked!

First he was sent to a prison for violent criminals, where nobody was allowed to talk because it was maxi-mum security!

Then he was sent to a hard labor penitentiary. The warden kept the convicts hauling heavy wagons up a steep hill in the hot sun with a stay-pulling gun! Ken hated it so much there, he tried to chew his way to freedom, but it was for gnawt!

Finally, after two years of good behavior, he was moved to a minimum security jail where he met some interesting people.

There was the burglar, who lamented that the cops had seized his favorite crowbar, his pried and joy!

A couple of swindlers taught him how to gain your victim's trust with con tact!

Six Chinese bears, who got arrested sitting in a circle and peacefully eating bamboo, because they were panda ring!

And a rain god, jailed in a case of mist taken identity.

But best of all, Ken met a woman prisoner and spent so much time with her, they felon love!

They were six weeks from freedom when a crazy inmate named John Van der Kloot started to harass Ken endlessly. Each time Ken calmly asked John to stop, but the madman hollered, "If you don't like it, kill me."

Although the idea appealed to Ken, he remained civil -- and called the guards. But they hauled him into court again -- for a tempted murder!

16. Grab Bag: Some of This & Some of That

Daffynitions

Ick-citable: Someone who gets enraged by grime and gunk!

Semi-colon: What's left after operating for intestinal cancer!

Incomepoop: Someone who judges you solely by how much money you make!

Capacity: How much head you can get into a hat!

Assassinnate: Person who's inherently doubly asinine!

Lewdicrous: X-rated movie with an improbable plot!

Die-jest: Summary of humor for undertakers!

Konkwest: Results of an armed invasion from the east that defeated the defending army by bopping them all on the head!

Seeductive: The way the flowers treat the bees!

Bickini: What a pen wears to the beach!

Wis-sconce-in: State where most lights are on the walls!

Mind over madder: The best way to control a wicked temper!

Gooffaw: When you laugh at someone else's big, huge mistake!

Official NoDice: Government refusal of your application to open a casino!

Abrupture: What happens when you lift a heavy weight too fast!

Slipshod: Wearing your lingerie on your feet!

Wannabees: Wasps that spend all their time wishing they could make honey!

Hellium: Devil's favorite gas!

Knee cap: Hat you put on your leg!

A meano acid: Nasty, misfolded, disease-causing protein!

A Hungarian demolition company hired a man from Prague as a subcontractor in charge of demolishing a trust company building. But when they came to inspect his work two weeks later, they found the Czech didn't clear the bank!

Why can't Congress get anything done?
Because they're a bunch of legis-laters!

Did you hear about the two little girl rocks that were formed from the same mother shale? They were schisters!

Why did the congregation think their minister saw evil everywhere? He was always saying, "Yes sindeed!

Why can't you take away the fancy carved wood surrounding the fireplace in a Victorian dwelling? You'll dis-mantle the house!

What's the leading cause of dismissal for accountants?
The wrong additude!

Why don't most politicians give you specifics when they talk?
They have over-developed vaguest nerves!

The moron did not worry when he dashed across a 10-lane freeway full of high-speed traffic. He had an auto-immune disease!

Why don't people want to buy shoes with the bottoms made from donkey leather, even though it's tough and long-wearing?
Because then they'd have two more ass soles!

What would you call a powder that turned a Norwegian into a native-born resident of Stockholm? Artificial Swedener!

The dirt around a hockey net is so valuable because it's goal dust!

Did you know that a huge meteorite hit the Southwest?
That's why there's a Denton Texas!

With all the lobbying money inundating Washington, we have a buy-partisan government!

Where do you get the longest-lasting work clothes?
At the hard wear store!

How many ways can the wind dry out a woman's lips?
  Chapped her 1
  Chapped her 2
  Chapped her 3 ....!

What kind of plastic window causes confusion? Perplexiglass!

The typical politician is not smart and he doesn't knowwit!

If you keep an acorn in your hand too long you get a palm tree!

Lindsay Lohan didn't make a formal speech when she was freed from jail --
  just some off-the-cuffs remarks!

Fallen-away Catholics are really parish-shunners!

What would you call the increasing use of sugar that crowds out nutrients in
  processed food? Dessertification!

Why should you take small, brownish birds into your house in blizzards?
  You should think of them as your chilled wrens!

How do you check to make sure a dress was properly altered?
  You put a small seam stress on it!

A Martian landed in the Mojave Desert, walked up to a single-serve Coke®
  bottle, and said "Take me to your liter!"

Judge Jeon actually admired contentious defendants.
  If they didn't contest his verdicts, he found them not appealing!

How many kinds of funeral dirges are there? Many varieties —
  they're die verse!

Why did Luke Skywalker rename his mentor when he stepped on a skunk?
  He de-Yoda-rized him!

What was the mathematician's reaction when a hidden short in his calculator
  made the add key subtract instead? He was nonplussed!

Why did the hospital payroll clerk think he was a physician?
  Because every time a nurse was late for work, the clerk told his boss,
  "I docked her, I docked her!"

Why did the moron bring half a beef carcass to chemistry class?
  He wanted to study ox sides!

What happens to someone with an upper leg replacement if they break dance too soon after their operation? They get a hip pop!

Someone who keeps dawdling when all his friends want to get going has no c'mon sense!

Filibusters are a highly specialized form of in-senate-y!

They don't allow white steer in the largest city in Turkey because Is tan bull!

Women are so much more productive in Myanmar because of the Road to Man delay!

Yuppies buy so much because they have developed highly new wants thinking!

What is the opposite of half-assed? Ass whole!

Gaston and Didianne Losofée, two practical, achievement-oriented businesspeople were perturbed their only son seemed to have his head in the clouds, and spent hours reading about obscure theoretical scholars. So they went to a psychologist, who said, "You should never have named him Phil!"

Why did the computer apply for a credit card? It got laid off in the Great Depression of 2010, and its cache was running low!

Why did the Russian national security agency breed clever, honey-making insects? It wanted very cagey bees!

Why is an ointment for treating skin problems on your butt out of-this-world? Because it's ass steroids!

What did Samuel Chen say about the recurring errors his accountant was making? "I'll have to hire sumbody else!"

Why does the glamorous woman in the green silk dress wear dark glasses? So you think she's looking into the distance, but she really has horizon you!

The fanciest seat of government in the world is a cap-it-all!

A very religious bee built a miniature chapel inside a flower.
He called it the Church of the In Carnation!

An independent trucker who delivers fasteners is like a tool because he's a screw driver!

What do you call a senator who sits on his butt and never does anything for anybody unless they bribe him? A politushan!

Why can't you mine for iron with a drill? It will go into ore-bit!

The mapmaker walked around barefoot because he was a toe-pographer!

In the 1477, there was a notorious livestock thief named Deodatus Morrow. When he stole the fat rabbit the Johnson family was going to eat for Sunday dinner, Old Man Johnson went to the sheriff, who said, "Hare today. Gone to Morrow!"

After 48 hours in labor, what did Diane Aluya name her newborn son? Hal!

What chemical should you never use in the woods of New England? Cause tick soda!

Do not ever ask a German for a favor at nein o'clock!

Why did the moron take his new prescription medicine to the Museum of Modern Art? He wanted to have it cure-rated!

What Irish city should Arnold Köhler stay away from no matter what? Killarney!

Will household dirt hurt me? Dust mite!

Why does smoke come out of James Papadopoulos' leg joint? Because that's where his Jim knee is!

GRAPE EXPECTATIONS

Joe the Grape lived a long and sinful life. He drank, gambled, used drugs, killed a whole bunch of other Grapes, lied, cheated, and was in and out of jail.

The grape sheriff finally shot and killed him during a bank robbery. When he woke up in a huge room filled with flames, a tall Grape with a pointed tail and a pitchfork came over to him.

"What happened? Where am I?" Joe the Grape asked.

"Don't worry," replied the tall Grape. "You'll be involved in raisin' hell for eternity!"

THEN THEY RE-TIRED

Three astronauts landed on Mars, very excited to be the first humans to visit the planet. They let down their spaceship's ramp, and drove their Marsmobile down onto the red desert.

Oohing and aahing at the sculptured rocks and undulating red sand dunes, they were having the time of their lives until two tires suddenly blew out.

The moment they stopped, a flying saucer glided up, and four little purple people jumped out.

"We're from earth," the head astronaut said. "Who are you?"

The purple guys grinned and said," We're good samartians!"

THEY SAID TO THE BANK: LIEN ON ME

Mirko and Sanya Bolic lived with his parents, even though they had three kids, they both worked, and the lack of privacy in the tiny flat drove them nuts! Finally, they were able to scrape together a down payment on a cottage of their own. When they got the mortgage, Mirko picked Sanya up in his arms and said, "Finally, a loan together!"

17. Guest Punster Showcases

Punderdome® 3000
Punderdome® Big Box Winners share their best!

Created and staged by Fred and Jo Firestone, an amazing father-daughter team of homespun comedians, the wonderfully hokey Punderdome® 3000 pun slam has played to packed houses in super-sophisticated Brooklyn, New York since 2011.

Each month, 18 contestants fight a war of wits designed to win the first and second Big Box prizes. The prizes, themselves, are funny. One recent Big Box had an old-fashioned 3-tiered bon-bon tray that looked like it came from Aunt Sadie's parlor, along with a luscious assortment of fresh fruit to display on it! Another had a brand new oak toilet seat and a plunger.

Each contestant chooses a Punderdome® name. The puns, on assigned topics, fly thick, fast, and funny, and about three hours later two skillful punsters are crowned First and Second Place winners.

If you want to visit a Punderdome® performance, plan ahead, because the show sells out and latecomers without tickets are out of luck. For more information about Punderdome®, see http://facebook.com/punderdome and http://punderdome.com You can buy tickets online, in advance, at http://www.littlefieldnyc.com/calendar.

PUNKY BREWSTER (A.K.A. "REKHA SHANKAR") is an improviser and comedy writer in New York. She is a producer/editor on the webseries, *LADYPOINTS*, which highlights artistic women who define success in their own terms. She is also an assistant editor for all those murder recreation shows you might watch in marathons on the weekend. You can see her work at: http://www.youtube.com/user/penguinsandfiber and http://ladypoints.tumblr.com/.

- No one knows it, but Eli Whitney was a notorious alcoholic. He was always caught in gin!

- *You* wrote that book about growing up in Louisiana. I don't care if you feel your editor helped you a lot. That memoir is bayou!

- Luck was on my side during my final argument in court: I got my client off of his sentence, off of parole, off of community service, and absolved of his monetary fine. It was a four-leafed closer.

- My doctor is a classic rock fan. So when I complained of stomach pains for hours after I ate a loaf of bread, he said, "So-Coeliac, it's making you fart, it's making you constipate daily!"

PUNTIUM PROCESSOR (A.K.A. "JEREMY PURSER) was a first-time 'Domer, contestant, and Big Box Champion at the April 2013 edition of Punderdome® 3000. He is a writer, comedian, and designer working and living in Brooklyn, NY. His work can be seen on his website www.jeremypurser. com.

- It only takes me a few strides to feel Runner's Sigh!

- Did you hear about the new restaurant in Brooklyn that puts a hip spin on Southern comfort food? It's a gentri-fried chicken place.

- "re: re: re: re: re: re: re: Respect" — Aretha Franklin's inbox

- I pit my literary friends against each other by telling them, "She doesn't hold a Kindle to you."

- There were only two doctors in my hometown. They asked all of their patients to stop smoking, but they were chain smokers themselves. That's a strange paradox.

THE NOAH CONSTRICTOR (A.K.A. "NOAH KLINGER") is a nonprofit fundraiser, amateur composer and aspiring diplomat originally from Washington DC. The first time he can remember laughing was because of a pun on the old *Transformers* cartoon show, and a lifetime obsession was born. To see his work, please ask nicely, or visit his very occasional blog at http://savingaeneas.blogspot.com/

- I failed my Communist geometry test; I forgot that Red Square has four right Engels!

- My uncle was a very devoted shepherd -- so much so that he stayed with his sheep right up until the moment of his death. I guess he was a real died-in-the-wool sort of guy!

- I wandered into a restaurant and ordered a baguette. The waiter told me, "This is an Indian restaurant. I'd like to give you a baguette, but we have naan!"

- An albino was arrested and demanded a jury of his peers. The judge said that finding 12 albinos would take a long time. The defendant, however, insisted on his right to a fair trial!

- A geometry teacher left for vacation a pale fellow, but after two weeks on the beach he returned a tan gent.

ANGEL LEON

Angel Leon is a software developer, entrepreneur, dad, and the creator of Punsr. com. You can follow him on Twitter at http://twitter.com/gubatron.

- *Nobel Prize:* Prize awarded to creator of the best knock-knock jokes!

- *Ground Beef:* Cow with no legs!

- *Lacerate:* The speed at which you tie your shoes!

- *Panicking:* The master of fear and anxiety!

- *Polygamist:* Game addicted parrot!

- *Amusing:* First person declaration of taking or consuming something!

- *Protectants:* What the Queen Ant orders the soldiers of the colony to do!

- *Aromatic:* Mechanical bow that shoots and reloads until it runs out of ammo

- *Remove:* To change position twice or more times!

- *Currency:* Electrically charged large body of salt water!

- *Eiffel Tower:* What the Pisa Tower will say if they don't take care of it!

- *Sublime:* Green submarine!

- *Mushroom:* Place to keep your cornmeal, grits or polenta!

- *Basically:* Essentially simple associate!

- *Bigamous:* Rodent of considerable size!

- *Release:* What your landlord wants you to do!

PAUL EGGLESTON

Paul Eggleston lives in Suffolk, England. He tweets silly jokes whenever he's not at work and his wife and kids let him. His puns can be seen by following @Pauleggleston on Twitter.

- Drills are the best tools in the hole whirled.

- Don't bother talking to me about fashion. It goes in one year, and out the other.

- Excavating chalk from Kent coastline cliffs sounds difficult, but its just mine Dover matter.

- I first met my wife at dawn one day when I stopped to give her car a push after she'd broken down. It was shove at first light.

- I bought my daughter's door from a daughter door salesman.

- The funniest two buttons on my keyboard are ,d

- My impersonation of a seat is, at best, am-a-chair-ish.

- My new "ridiculously oversized bucket for getting water out of a hole in the ground" invention hasn't gone down well.

- If you want to slow a seagull down you're going to have to weight your tern.

- My wife says I'm an idiot for buying this invisible magazine. I can't see the issue.

- My mate screwed some insurance paperwork up into a ball and knocked 10 skittles over with it. That's a bowled claim.

- I must stop waving incense around when I talk. I always get told off for jossstickulating too much.

- My mate is worried that his head has quite a distinct taper towards the top. And I can see his point.

O. Henry Pun-Off

World Champion punsters
share their favorites!

The O. Henry Pun-Off is probably the oldest continual pun contest in the world, dating back to 1978. The annual event is held each May at the O. Henry Museum in Austin Texas, and gets international press coverage.

Produced and hosted by former champion punster Gary Hallock, the contest has two divisions. *The Punslingers* matches contestants' wits on assigned topics. Pairs of contestants have a five count to come up with puns on that topic, as they volley back and forth. Winners from each of several pairings go up against each other until a champion is declared.

Punniest of Show gives contestants up to 90 seconds to present a pun-filled narrative on stage. A panel of judges rates each contestant on content, originality, and audience response.

You can find out more about the O. Henry Pun-Off at http://punpunpun. com, and http://www.facebook.com/PUNYPAGE. You can also see videos of O. Henry World Champions in action at http://bit.ly/11a4QMQ.

BENJAMIN ZIEK has always been in love with puns. A hotel night auditor by trade, he has won the O. Henry Pun-Off World Championship four times, including a double win in the 2013 Punslingers *and* Punniest of Show competitions. You can follow him on twitter @punmanben, and see a video of his 2010 O. Henry championship performance at http://bit.ly/18xZ4cQ.

- Did you hear about the Amish girl who was so popular she dated ten Mennonite?

- I brought my sister to the British Billiards Club, but they said she was too young to enter. Well, don't tell anyone, but I snooker in.

- After breakfast, I became really good with words, but I had to pick wooden splinters out of my mouth all day. That's the last time I'll eat Scrabbled eggs!

- Hey! Stop trying to steal my building blocks… Lego!

- Did you hear about the nursery rhyme character who loved cabbage? It was Old King Coleslaw!

- I love toffee. I write down every toffee bar I have eaten in my Heath Ledger!

- A lipstick and a mascara tried to enter a bar, but the female bartender said they had to leave. The lipstick replied, "But we already paid the Cover, Girl!"

- What did the arthritic ranch hand say after taking the baby horses for a 5 mile walk? "Oh, my ponies!"

- If you have curly hair, you night not want to go to a park or beach where a lot of people are playing, because you might get stung by Frisbees!

KIRK MILLER is a retired IT Professional who was introduced to puns by his stepfather, his mentor. Kirk became a tormentor, much to the chagrin of his wife and others. As his stepfather said: "If a pun is the lowest form of humor, then it must be the *foundation* of humor." Kirk lives in Richardson, Texas, and likes to write limericks, especially ones with puns. Kirk won Punniest of Show in 2009 for this routine:

My father urged me to be a simple carpenter because carpenters are just **plane** folks. He said that when the drill bit was invented, it was a real **turning point**. He **drilled** it into me, but I thought it was **boring**. I would rather **tool** around with my friends.

The **unvarnished** truth is that I had a few **screws** loose and was **mallet**-justed. I had a drinking problem, and got **plastered** on **screwdrivers** with my friend **jack hammer** all the time.

One night my parents found me **hammered**, and that didn't **augur** well one **bit** with them. I wanted to **bolt** out of there. I made some dis**jointed** remarks and shouted, "Just **lathe** me alone!"

"Don't **razor** voice at me!" said Dad. He became **unhinged**! He **clamped** down on me, and finally I **saw** that I couldn't su**stain** that lifestyle. Yes, I **solder** light.

I tried to **square** things with Dad, so I joined a **splinter** group of Alcoholics Anonymous and **wrenched** myself away from booze. My sponsor said that I was en**dowel**ed with talent, and if I **joined** my dad's business, that everything **woodwork** out. He **chiseled** away at me until I decided to **joist** do it.

It was back to the old **grind**. It was a **riveting** experience as I **bore** down and had to **ratchet** up a notch. At first, I learned through **trowel** and error, but **ladder** on I finally **nailed** the **nuts** and **bolts** of the business.

So now I'm a **level**-headed man who is **vise** president. My father thinks that I am a real **knife** guy -- in fact, a **stud**. He is proud of me, and said, "When I **die**, son, this **awl** will be yours."

ANDY BALINSKY competes annually in the O. Henry Punoff. He's a graduate of Harvard's Comp Sci and Coldtowne Theater's improv programs. He likes wordplay, bird photography, and traveling in wild places.

2004 Election: One Bard Underhand is Worth Doin' It ta Bush

I'm **heron** this day to **grouse** about the **loons** who **Wood Duck** responsibility for the un**Pheasant** news from **Pauraque**. They **Thrushed** us into a **Swift War-bler**ring the truth. It has now taken a **Veery** nasty **Tern**. **Shrikes!** Those photos **Stilt** make me **Finch**. Are they **Raven** mad? And **Goose** who pays the **bill**? **Ptarmigan** and **ptarmigan**. **Waddle** be **nest**?

Don't they know America is only **Partridge** and mostly **Poor**? Will they be **Robin** and **Tealing** and never **Sparrow** dime?

It made my wife **Bittern**; a real **Blue bird**. But I said, "**Lark** here, **Starling**, don't be **Blue, Jay**. We'll **Magpies** and bake **Cuckoos** for democracy. We'll **Hawk** them, and raise some **Green-back' Here-on**." Well, **migrate** idea had her **grackling** a smile and **Crowing, Eagle** to begin. Now, she's **Hummingbird** songs.

Wren will this **Junco** end? Let **Osprey** it's **Owl** over **Vireo** soon. On Election Day, let's say, "**Bush, tit the Road! Runner** way! **Snowy Egrets**." So, ask me for a Voter Registration **Card-inal** give you one. **Vulture** do it for the birds?

STEVE BROOKS: Cross two guys named Brooks - Garth and Mel - and you get Austin folksinger Steve Brooks. His Garth side writes songs for Americana singers like Slaid Cleaves and Russell Crowe, while his Mel side won the O. Henry Pun-Off six times. Find songs and puns at www.stevebrooks.net.

Steve wrote this winning pun routine for the 2001 O. Henry Pun-Off World Championship[1], inspired by then-President Bush's repeated refusal to state whether he had ever used cocaine during what he called his "irresponsible youth." Which might help to explain why he sent 130,000 young Americans looking for weapons of mass destruction in Iraq:

My **Kilo** Americans. Let me **Freak** to you about a **Homegrown** Texan, who has **Resin** to the Highest **Possession** in this great **Hallucination**, the **original Come-Pushing-It** conservative, the **Pass-the-Hemp** of the **Fume-Lighted States**, George Dubya **Bushel**.

He grew up near the **Mescaline** border. These days, he's **Hippie-Critical**, but **Ounce** upon a time, he was a **Peyote** animal. A-**Codeine** to some sources, he once had a **Morphine** violation, but his **Poppy Baled** him out, and it never made the **Papers**. He studied **Acid**-uously, earned his **LSD**, and graduated **Ganga** cum **Loaded**.

Then he came home to **Marijuana** those Texas girls. Soon, opportunity **Narced**: a **Grass**-roots run for the **Opiate** Office. His campaign **Stoners** gave **Sinsemilla Dealers, Amphetamine** to **IV** advertising.

But election day was a **Heroin** experience. The votes were evenly **Spliff**. The lead **Zig-Zagged** for weeks. It was **Reefer Count Madness!** But thanks to the Supreme **Snort**, he won by a **Nose**.

He's still **Burning the Ropes** of the job, with help from Colin **Powder**, former Head of the the **Joint Sheafs** of **Stash**. They're trying to **Psychedelic**-ate balance between **Tokes** cuts for the **Roach**, and helping the **Needles**, while **Cheeching** kids to **Weed**, by giving **Tracks** dollars to the **Free Methodist Prayer Force**.

He's on a **Roll**, and we're all sitting on **Ecstasy** what he's **Cocaine** up next. So when you hear "**Inhale** to the Chief," just say **Snow**.

---

[1] Copyright © 2001 by Steve Brooks and Frog Records. Used by permission.

GARY HALLOCK competed in and won medals in the O. Henry Pun-Off World Championships in Austin, Texas for 5 years -- and then became the producer and emcee. Since 1990, the contest, under his guidance, has thrived and groan to become the word-clash event it is today. Trade puns with him at www.punpunpun.com and/or www.facebook.com/punypage.

- I ordered my eggs "sunny side up" but the waitress brought them "scrambled." This is something I will not get over easy.

- The best way to make sure you have your ducts in a row is to take preventive measures.

- A placebo is nearly the same as a gazebo except that it has no roof. Your medical insurance won't cover it.

- Did you hear about the Kodiak ursine whose cubs were always breech births? She never could get her bearing straight.

- I can't stop shoplifting instruments to perform pedicures. I may be a clip toe maniac.

- When you visit the chiropractor, bring your own magazines to read while you wait. What they'll have there are mostly back issues.

- A pun is the shortest distance between two straight lines.

- And probably the lightest vehicle ever made would also be a British car. One MG.

- Ephemeral: A Public Radio station that quickly goes bankrupt.

- Brother: Sibling who helps make the soup.

- Oliver Twist: What the bartender asks when you order your martini.

- Once spawn a time you wrote that salmon won't lay eggs twice. However some larger species do, and can easily accomplish tuna roe.

STAN KEGEL is a retired pediatric cardiologist who is a leading advocate in popularizing puns on the internet. In 2000, he was awarded "Punster of the Year" by the International Save the Pun Foundation. His postings appear in over 30 joke lists, and he is the senior judge at the annual O. Henry International Pun-Off. To subscribe to his free "Puns" joke list send a blank email to puns-subscribe@yahoogroups.com, and for "Jest For Kids" for 8-to-14-year-olds, e-mail jest4kids-subscribe@yahoogroups.com.

THE ARCHEOLOGISTS

Two archeologists, exploring a remote mountain in Tibet came across a huge granite statue which resembled a sitting man. It stood almost 400 foot tall, and its bodily details were accurate down to the fingernails and teeth. "It looks real enough to talk," says one. "Let's try," says the other and turning to the statue asks it its name. No answer. "How old are you?" No answer. Finally, one shouts out, "What is the square root of 64?"

Suddenly, the mountain shakes as the giant statue rises onto its feet and puts its hand on its chin. Then after about ten seconds, the statue answers in a roaring voice, "Eight." "Of course, says the scientist, "It only stands to reason."

THE BURGLAR

It is Christmas Eve. A burglar breaks into the home of a prominent local lawyer. He takes the lawyer's Christmas gifts from under the tree leaving the packages for the wife and children alone. As he is leaving the house, he is apprehended by a policeman.

He confesses to what he has done but tells the policeman that he can't be arrested. The policeman asks why, and he responds, "Because the law states that I'm entitled to the presents of an attorney."

Punsr

David Yale's favorites from punsr!

Punsr is an online, ongoing punning contest, with thousands of players throughout the world. You can submit your puns either by Twitter, using the hashtag #punsr, or at their website: www.punsr.com.

The format for Punsr submissions is simple: #punsr WORD: Funny punny definition goes here.

Players get points for each pun, and even more points for puns with memes (illustrations). When other Punsr players re-tweet your pun, you get additional points. Re-tweeting other players' puns also yields you points.

The players with the most retweet points each week get top rankings, and all players can arrange to get part of the Google ad revenue for their memes, Punsr's, and profile page.

When you submit a pun to Punsr, it becomes part of their pun dictionary, with each entry credited to its creator. This is the biggest pun dictionary in the world, and a great way to see if anyone else has already come up with puns you're thinking about.

You can see Punsr's favorite memes at http://instagram.com/punsr#. To see more puns from Showcase participants, go to their Punsr websites, listed on the following pages.

@AFerenbach - Dr. Drew Bach (a.k.a. Dr. Andrew Ferenbach) http://www. punsr.com/tweep/?t=aferenbach

- Lubricate: What comes after brick seven and before brick nine in outdoor toilet construction!

- Impudent: The supernatural being that you hit with your car!

- Rambler: What you see when a male sheep runs past you at spectacular speed!

- Update: An evening out that is so exciting, you don't need a blue pill!

- Hairspray: What the things growing out of your head do when they see the scissors coming!

- Cutaneous: What you get if you sit down on broken glass!

- Considerations: Thinking about Army food!

@VChatting (a.k.a Vidisha Chatterjee) http://www.punsr.com/tweep/?t=vchatting

- Pretence: The time before you learnt grammar!

- Passionfruit: The one you gave birth to!

- Condone: Theft accomplished!

- Announcer: Responding to teacher's question about parts of speech with, "A noun Sir!"

- Zealot: Reference to the frequent usage of the last letter of the English alphabet!

- Sometimes: Specific moments in the study of Mathematics when you practise addition!

@MumblingNerd (a.k.a. Roy Manterfield)
http://www.punsr.com/tweep/?t=mumblingnerd
http://mumblingnerd.com

- Hatred: Father Christmas's headwear!

- Undercapitalise: Infrequent use of initial upper-case letters!

- Livelihood: Active gangster!

- Speculate: Belated glasses!

- Sociopath: The route to Twitter!

- Duopoly: Two simultaneous games of Monopoly!

- Generator: Person who evaluates genes!

- Procrastinating: Progression from amateurcrastinating!

- Pirate: Pie classification system!

- Nottingham: Tying bacon!

- Gruntled: When a piglet gets its voice!

- Granary: Warehouse to store grandmothers!

@i_theindian (a.k.a. Deep Banerjee)
http://www.punsr.com/tweep/?t=i_theindian
www.thepunliners.blogspot.in

- Adore: Increase the mineral content!

- Exit-poll: What firefighters use when responding to an alarm!

- Adduce: Append two!

- Outweigh: Exit!

- Boron: Keep drilling!

- Doctorate: What the medical practitioner did when served food!

- Macarena: Showcase for Apple computers!

- Clones: Are people two!

THE PUN RUN
FOUNDER BEC HILL'S BEST PUNS!

Britain's only pun-based comedy night was founded by Aussie comedian Bec Hill and is co-run by Gavin J. Innes and Little Red Noise Production House.

Pun Run has been such a smashing success they've had to move to a larger venue and split into two shows. The original Pun Run, which showcases more established comedians, is held every other month. Pun Size, a new show for fresh comics and Pun Run favorites is a chance to try out new (pun-based) material, and is held in alternate months. Both shows are in London.

The shows feature many styles of pun-based comedy, from zingy one-liners to pun stories and pun skits complete with props.

For more information, see http://facebook.com/thepunrun. To hear acts from PunRun go to https://soundcloud.com/punrun. You can follow them on Twitter @ThePunRun and you can follow Bec Hill @BecHillComedian.

- I ain't sayin' she's a gold digger: just that she's a minor.
- I run the best convent nightclub out there: Bar Nun.
- Deck chairs. But only in self defence.
- That's the third bap I've sat on today. I'm on a roll.
- Have you tried light aircraft? They're a little plane.
- I love my abacus. You can always count on it.

About the Author

From an interview by Carrie Smoot, originally published on her website, http://carriesbookshelf.wordpress.com/. Reprinted with permission.

Tell me a little bit about your career. Are you still a public relations guy?

My first career was as a college instructor during graduate school in Minnesota, teaching freshman communication. I did dramatic things in class to make my point, including taking my suit jacket and trousers off. (I had jeans and a work shirt underneath!) Years later, when I hear from former students, they still have vivid memories of my classes.

After graduation, I ran a neighborhood recreation program in North Minneapolis for the Parks Department. Among other things, I worked with a large group of teenagers, often making up silly songs on the spot to make my point with them.

I moved to California, got a part-time job with Oakland Parks & Recreation as a consultant, and was quickly promoted and trained as a public relations officer. My secret dream had come true—I was actually being paid to write.

At the time, there were no good books and no adult education classes about PR for people involved in nonprofit organizations. I started teaching seminars for the University of California, first in Berkeley, and soon after, throughout the state. At one of my seminars, a literary agent in the audience suggested I write a book, and offered to represent me. That's how my first book, *The Publicity Handbook*, was born. It's still in print today, 31 years later, and was a Fortune Book Club selection.

But I was homesick for New York, even after many years away. So I moved back here, rented a tiny office on Fifth Avenue, and set up a freelance writing practice. A number of clients asked me to write direct mail promotions, and I discovered I loved them far better than public relations.

After staff positions with Publishers Clearing House and Lindenwold Fine Jewelers, I returned to freelancing. I have clients in the USA, Canada, Australia, England, and Germany, and I regularly teach direct marketing seminars in Germany.

How did you get interested in puns and wordplay?

There were two big influences. First of all, I always heard things differently than other people in my family. When I was about six, my dad told me he had gotten a raise in pay. I was quite upset. "Dad, we can't eat all those raisins. We need money!" I said. I didn't know it then, but I was hearing the words as a mondegreen, a misinterpretation that is a form of punning.

The other big influence was my uncle, Arthur Gordon. Artie loved puns and jokes, which he always told in a quiet, understated, and very funny manner. He'd tell a pun, my dad would laugh until tears rolled down his cheeks, and I, at the age of seven or eight, sometimes didn't get it. But Uncle Artie would patiently explain the pun to me until I *did* get it. And then, at a later date, he would retell it so I would get a chance to laugh at it, too.

My interest in words continued to grow. When I was in fifth grade, I discovered that the East New York Savings Bank had a newsletter for kids—and it published poetry. I promptly submitted some of mine and it got published. I was hooked on words.

By the time I was a teenager, I was punning all the time, and it was a wonderful outlet for the typical adolescent wiseguy I was.

What inspired you to write books on humor and punning?

When I worked at Publishers Clearing House, I was continually punning. That's when I started writing down my puns on slips of paper—and keeping them. Several friends there urged me to put them into book form. I did, but even though I was a published book author with an agent, I couldn't get it published. Years later, I looked at the manuscript again, realized it was really good, gave it another try, and voilà! *Pun Enchanted Evenings* was born.

How do you come up with puns? What is your thought process?

It just happens. I don't usually think about it at all. Sometimes they just pop into my head, fully formed. And sometimes I hear other people talking, and misinterpret the words as mondegreens. Recently, I was in a coffee shop eating lunch. Two men at the next table were talking, and one of them got moderately upset. "Don't take offense," the other guy said, but I didn't hear it that way. "There aren't any fences in here to be taken," I said in a stage whisper. But they both heard me—started laughing—and forgot about the upset.

Another time, I was walking in Manhattan. A big burly guy was delivering kegs of ale, but he didn't have a hand truck. So he was carrying them, one at a time, and I could hear the ale sloshing. When he put down the keg, without even thinking, I went up to him and said, "Do you know you're a poet?" "I am? Why?" he asked. "Because you shakes beer!" We both had a good laugh.

Since I can't predict when they'll pop into my head, and I forget them if I don't write them down, I have to keep pads and pens everywhere—in my coat pocket, on the kitchen table, in the bathroom, and on my nightstand along with a flashlight. I sometimes wake up during the night, use the flashlight so I don't disturb my wife, and write down a pun I was dreaming about.

Do you write a lot of them at once, and then test them out on your family? How do you know you have a keeper? Is it a little like stand-up comedy?

Some days—even some weeks—I don't come up with any puns at all. And then there are the super-productive days when I create as many as 37 of them. My rule of thumb is that I *always* write them down on my pads, no matter how bad or rudimentary they are. Often what I write down first is just the idea.

When I have a bunch of puns on my pads, I go to my computer to put them into my database. That's when I shape them and research them. I want to make sure I'm using words correctly and have my facts right—especially after I realized—*after* it was published—that I had made a factual error in *Pun Enchanted Evenings*. Pun #153 refers to a gnu as a bird. It is not any such thing! Although the error does not kill the pun, I'm embarrassed that I didn't know a gnu is an African antelope, not a bird.

One thing that amazes me is that people choose different puns as their favorites. Both on Twitter (judging by which puns get retweeted) and in reviews of the book, there is little agreement about which puns are favorites.

I do try out my puns on family and friends. My wife likes some, but not all of them, but my 18-year-old daughter abhors them all. I've also tried performing them, and yes, it is a little bit like stand-up comedy.

What are the characteristics of great, effective, and memorable puns?

Great puns surprise you with a punch line you don't expect. They are funny, and they often reveal a bit of truth that some people may even find uncomfortable. My favorite, which I wrote recently: "People who want to slash education budgets won't take know for an answer!"

IF YOU REALLY LIKE THIS BOOK

Thank you for reading *HomesPun Humor*. I hope you enjoyed many good giggles and belly laughs! I'd love to hear your reactions, comments, praise, criticisms, and anything else you have to say. You can write to me at David@ BestPuns.Com.

If you really love this book, please help spread the word and help this punster keep punning!

1. Tell your friends, and wheedle, cajole, and inveigle them to buy their own copies of the paperback or eBook version at www.bestpuns.com/ buy1. If they're not ready to buy, tell them to follow me on Twitter @Bestpuns, where they'll get a regular flow of puns from both *HomesPun Humor* and *Pun Enchanted Evenings*.

2. Tweet, blog, or post a note about *HomesPun Humor* on Facebook.

3. If you know an editor, reporter, blogger, radio or TV personality, tell them about *HomesPun Humor*. Let them know they can get a free review copy by emailing the publisher: media@aHealthyRelationship.Com.

4. Ask your local library to order a copy. Please give them the ISBN number for the paper version: ISBN 978-0-9791766-7-8, the url: www.bestpuns. com/ librarians-bookstores.html, and the publisher's unique identifying number, SAN 852-6958. Please tell them the book is distributed by Ingram.

5. Link to www.bestpuns.com on your website. You may quote up to 20 Yale puns on your website, providing credit is given to *HomesPun Humor* by David R. Yale and www.bestpuns.com.

6. Write a review of *HomesPun Humor* on Amazon.com, Amazon.ca, Amazon.co.uk, or for your favorite website or print publication.

7. *HomesPun Humor* makes a wonderful, inexpensive gift. Give your friends and loved ones the gift of laughter, with their very own copies of *HomesPun Humor*.

8. If you're a member of a club, group, or organization whose members love puns, arrange for a live visit with David R. Yale. I'm available in person in the Washington to Boston area, and by Skype anywhere in the world. You can contact me at David@BestPuns.Com.

9. Use *HomesPun Humor* to raise funds for your organization! Discounts up to 50% off list price are available on quantity purchases over 10 copies.

10. Give your clients and customers the gift of giggles with *HomesPun Humor*. Discounts up to 50% off list price are available on quantity purchases over 10 copies, and for large orders over 500 copies, your business' name can be imprinted on the cover.

11. If you haven't read *Pun Enchanted Evenings: 746 Original Word Plays* yet, buy a copy of the paperback or the eBook at: www.bestpuns.com/buy1.

Thank you for all you do.

– David R. Yale, Author
Pun Enchanted Evenings
David@BestPuns.Com

For information on other pun resources, including books, websites, and Twitter feeds, go to http://www.bestpuns.com/puninfo.html

If you liked *HomesPun Humor,* don't miss…

Pun Enchanted Evenings:
746 Original Word Plays
A Treasury of Wit, Wisdom, Chuckles & Belly Laughs
for Language Lovers

By David R. Yale
The Pundit of Double Entendres

746 wildly original puns on every subject from Arizona to zealous crusaders!

More than a half a dozen ant puns certain to start a new fad!

Bi-lingual puns in English and Spanish, French, Chinese, Latin!

The best new moron puns since the Fifties!

You'll laugh out loud – guaranteed!

Plus information on the first scientific studies
to show the mental superiority of pun-lovers!

Winner of the
2011 Global eBook Award for Comedy & Humor

Available Worldwide
108 Pages, Paper: ISBN 978-0-9791766-4-7
Kindle eBook: ISBN 978-0-9791766-6-1

See where to get your copy at:
http://www.bestpuns.com/buy1.html

CPSIA information can be obtained at www.ICGtesting.com
Printed in the USA
BVOW05s2015280815

415153BV00004B/251/P